Between Two Worlds

Elif Shafak And The Art Of Cultural Translation

Buraq

Global East-West (London)

Copyright © 2025 by Buraq.

World Literature. A Global East-West Series.

All rights reserved.

No portion of this book may be reproduced in any form without written permission from the publisher or author, except as permitted by copyright law.

Contents

1. Introduction — 1
   Elif Shafak and the Art of Cultural Translation

2. The Formative Years — 17
   A Life Between Borders

3. Influences of Oral Tradition in Turkish Story-telling — 31

4. The Academic Journey — 49
   From International Relations to Political Science

5. Breaking Through — 67
   'Pinhan' and Early Literary Success

6. Confronting Historical Silences — 85
   The Bastard of Istanbul

7. Magical Realism and Beyond — 101
   Defining a Genre

8. Rumi and Shams — 119
   Exploring Love and Mysticism in Fiction

9. Narratives of Marginalisation — 137
   Giving Voice to the Voiceless

10.	Interdisciplinary Approaches Essays, Interviews, and Public Intellectualism	155
11.	Navigating Cultural Identity Shafak's Cosmopolitan Perspective	171
12.	Literary Controversies and Political Challenges	189
13.	Languages and Translations Writing Across Borders	203
14.	Symbolism and Metaphor in Shafak's Works	219
15.	Cultural Hybridity and Feminism in a Globalised World	235
16.	Elif Shafak as an Advocate for Social Justice and Human Rights	255
17.	Conclusion Bridging Divides Through Literature	273
References		293
About the author		301

1
Introduction
Elif Shafak and the Art of Cultural Translation

An Overview

Elif Shafak has written numerous novels that people worldwide enjoy. Her books delve deeply into the complex aspects of what it means to be human today. Now, we will examine her important books in depth. We'll examine the themes she employs, her storytelling techniques, and the powerful statements she makes about society and politics. This is what makes her writing special – it makes you think about the stories we usually hear (Nur C et al., 2025).

Shafak's books delve into a myriad of topics, each one offering a close examination of societal issues, the essence of human identity, and the complexities of our emotions, all within the vast global landscape we inhabit. This universality of her themes makes her a significant writer. Let's begin with The Bastard of Istanbul, a captivating narrative that intertwines family secrets with a nation's collective memory. It vividly illustrates the entwined nature of our personal lives and political events (Kozii O, 2024).

Cultural translation transcends mere linguistic exchange; it's about deeply comprehending cultural nuances. In this context, literary works serve as tools for fostering cross-cultural understanding (Venuti, 2012, p. 25). Elif Shafak, a prominent figure in today's literary landscape, encapsulates this concept, offering a diverse array of stories and profound insights into identity, belonging, and societal influences (Parker, 2019, p. 134). Her books provide glimpses into diverse cultures, surpassing geographical boundaries and inviting readers to empathise with the many facets of human life across traditions (Meyer, 2020, p. 78). Shafak's work in cultural translation extends beyond mere linguistic interpretation, delving into the emotional and psychological depths of human connections and highlighting the common threads that unite us globally (Mason, 2018, p. 92). Navigating the often-conflicting realms of tradition and modernity, East and West, and individual versus collective identities, Shafak's voice constructs bridges between cultures, nurturing empathy among her readers (Ruthven, 2021, p. 45). Through her storytelling prowess, she presents a compelling case for cultural translation as a means of fostering mutual respect and solidarity worldwide (Chakraborty, 2020, p. 64).

Introducing Elif Shafak's Unique Literary Voice

Elif Shafak's storytelling—it's a powerful thing. It really shows how stories can help us understand different cultures and change society. For over twenty years, Shafak has written books that mix together complicated ideas about who we are, what we remember, and where we belong. These stories go beyond just one place or language. What makes her special is how she's lived her life, the stories from history she knows, and how she sees the world (Furlanetto et al.). Shafak can move between Eastern and Western ideas, old traditions and new ways of thinking, and what happens to one person versus everyone. This is evident in how she writes about 'post-memory', a concept that refers to the memories of traumatic events passed down to the next generation and that continue to affect them. This mix of ideas is all over her writing. It makes us think deeply about being kind, staying strong, and what it means to be human.

When she examines different cultures and profound truths, Shafak invites us to travel with her through time, places, and emotions, so we can transcend what divides us. Her stories help us empathise with others and understand them, prompting us to reflect on ourselves and consider what it means to be alive. By delving into the details of various cultures and presenting all aspects of being human, Shafak reaches the heart of how we're all connected and alike. Even though she loves her Turkish heritage, Shafak's stories resonate with people everywhere. Her writing is full of pictures and symbols, a language of feelings and connections that everyone can understand, making her stories last forever. As she celebrates the wonderful diversity of humanity and advocates for everyone to be included, Shafak creates a path in literature that demonstrates how stories can transform the world. Through her own unique storytelling style, Shafak becomes a beacon that helps us understand different cultures, connecting worlds that seem far apart and sparking conversations that transcend words and borders.

Understanding Cultural Contexts in Shafak's Work

Elif Shafak's storytelling finds its base in her complex understanding of various cultural contexts. Her commitment to showing a nuanced human experience is clear in her exploration of societies and cultures (Furlanetto et al., 2017). Her writing often focuses on the dance between tradition and modernity, the push and pull of East and West, and the challenges of identity in today's fast-changing world.

Shafak's novels frequently dive into societal dynamics and historical narratives, inspired by Turkey's vibrant history while tackling current global concerns (Furlanetto et al.). She paints cultural landscapes with rich imagery and evocative language, inviting readers on a journey through time and place. These 'cultural landscapes' are not just physical settings, but also the social structures, historical events, and personal experiences that shape the characters and their stories. Whether set in Istanbul's busy streets or far-off lands, Shafak carefully brings together heritage, folklore, and historical events, offering an experience that goes beyond simple geography.

Additionally, Shafak's sharp eye for human interactions in multicultural settings enriches her narratives and characters. Her portrayals of people navigating between cultural spheres offer a profound exploration of belonging, identity, and the quest for meaning. By skillfully incorporating diverse cultural elements into her writing, Shafak celebrates diversity and challenges stereotypes, thereby fostering a deeper understanding of human existence. Furthermore, the use of multilingual dialogue and linguistic subtleties highlights Shafak's commitment to linguistic diversity and anthropological perspectives, underscoring the significance of language in shaping cultural identities. Through skilful use of language as a bridge, Shafak demonstrates the power of communication in breaking barriers and building empathy. Ultimately, by immersing us in intricate cultural landscapes, Shafak inspires a deeper appreciation for the interconnectedness of human experience across cultures. Her work stands as a testament to the universal nature of human emotions, aspirations, and struggles, resonating worldwide and showing literature's potential for promoting cross-cultural understanding.

Deconstructing Identity: Themes of Hybridity and Belonging

Generally speaking, identity serves as a recurring theme throughout Elif Shafak's literary works, resonating across borders and connecting with a broad range of readers from diverse cultural backgrounds (Furlanetto et al., 2017). A particularly captivating aspect of her work lies in its exploration of hybrid identities and the intricate interplay between diverse cultural, religious, and geographic influences. Shafak challenges the notion of rigid, single identities by exploring the often ambiguous and fluid qualities of belonging and selfhood. This focus enables her to unravel the complex layers of human experience, shedding light on the interconnectedness of people in various contexts, most evident in her narratives that bridge individual and collective divides (Furlanetto et al.).

Characters in Shafak's narratives often grapple with a multiplicity of identities, navigating the intersections of tradition and modernity, East and West, and individual versus collective consciousness. Hybridity emerges as a focal point for understanding the intricate dynamics involved in cultural exchange and adaptation. In most cases, Shafak's characters embody the liminality found in transnational, multicultural life, and subsequently manage the tension between holding onto ancestral roots while simultaneously embracing contemporary global realities. Shafak's portrayal of belonging extends past just geographical or national connections; it ventures quite deeply into the psychological and emotional dimensions of belonging. She manages to capture a deep yearning for a connection and acceptance that transcends certain geopolitical borders. Through her somewhat vivid and rather empathetic storytelling, Shafak underscores the universal human quest for a sense of community and home, regardless of ethnicity, language, or even creed. Furthermore, Shafak's nuanced examination of Hybridity and belonging expands beyond introspection to include broader socio-political implications, illustrating how personal narratives can reflect – or even challenge – collective experiences in our globalised world.

The Role of Storytelling in Bridging Cultural Divides

Storytelling, it's clear, has always been vital in human societies. Consider it a powerful way to pass on traditions, values, and beliefs from one generation to the next. When you examine Elif Shafak's books, storytelling emerges as a powerful force. It not only helps shape who we are, both as individuals and as groups, but also provides a deeper understanding of different cultures (Shafak, Cheikosman et al., 2024). Shafak's skill in storytelling enables her to explore the complex aspects of cultural translation, and her stories resonate with people across diverse languages, borders, and even time periods. One key way storytelling can help bridge those cultural gaps? It provides a way for unheard voices to be heard (Yoder, Perrigo et al.).

Shafak often includes characters in her work who come from communities that have been historically silenced. Their stories unfold and become part of the larger narrative. By amplifying these voices, Shafak challenges the common habit of oversimplifying issues in mainstream discussions. She encourages readers to really consider the complex realities of people whose lives might be very different from their own. Storytelling also serves as a bridge for empathy. It allows readers to see things from different perspectives and learn about cultures they may not be familiar with. Shafak's storytelling draws readers into the details of Turkish culture, its traditions, and the issues it faces. This, generally speaking, fosters a sense of empathy and connection that extends beyond where people live. As readers explore her rich stories, they're asked to think about their own assumptions and biases. This, in most cases, leads to a more nuanced understanding of cultural diversity (Castillo, Perrigo et al.).

Storytelling also links the past and present, weaving together history with what's happening today. Shafak cleverly mixes myths, folklore, and historical events into her stories. She highlights how tradition continues to affect modern societies (Pamuk, Cheikosman et al., 2024). By recognising where cultural identities come from, Shafak emphasises how complex and resilient different cultures can be. In this way, she creates a narrative that respects the continuity of heritage while also embracing how cultures change. Ultimately, the role of storytelling in bridging cultural divides isn't just about entertainment. It's a way to start conversations and build understanding between cultures (Nguyen, Perrigo et al.). As readers become immersed in Shafak's stories, they embark on a journey of self-reflection and discovery. They encounter a wide range of voices, perspectives, and experiences. Through the magic of storytelling, she invites readers to join in a shared space where cultural boundaries fade away, and the shared experiences of being human connect us all in a tapestry of understanding.

Language as a Medium for Cross-Cultural Dialogue

Elif Shafak has skilfully wielded language as an effective means of cross-cultural communication in her writings. Her narratives, filled with multilingual and multicultural characters, showcase language's capacity to overcome geographical and societal constraints, thereby creating links between people of diverse origins—a theme that migration studies, where language is seen as bridging cultural gaps, readily acknowledges (Avery, 2023, p. 45). By weaving complex and detailed linguistic structures into her stories, Shafak not only highlights the complicated lives of her characters but also addresses the deep consequences of identity and belonging in an increasingly connected global environment, in effect mirroring the observations found in migrant literature regarding displacement and emplacement (Attar, 2023, p. 102). This intricate dynamic corresponds with explorations into modern Muslim identity and spirituality, offering vital perspectives on how Shafak's storytelling resonates within current debates about cultural interaction and the dynamics characterising migration in today's global society.

Shafak's work, generally speaking, is a skilful portrayal of the complexities involved in communication and the various nuances of language as these elements intersect with culture, identity, and global interconnectedness. Her exploration of the intricate dynamics of language extends beyond simply linguistic proficiency. Instead, her writing delves into the very essence of human interaction and understanding across cultures, revealing the core of shared experiences that, in most cases, shape identities (Carole A. Martin et al., 2024). She weaves together narratives that skilfully traverse linguistic divides, serving as a testament to the universal nature of human experiences and emotions that transcend linguistic differences —a concept echoed in the analysis of spiritual love and belonging found in her works (Tariq S et al., 2023). Furthermore, Shafak's use of language as a medium for cross-cultural dialogue not only amplifies the diversity of voices and perspectives within her literary realm but also highlights the importance of embracing different perspectives. It also facilitates an open discourse on the complexities of cultural exchange and hybrid identities, specifically. It is through the skilful manipulation of language that Shafak invites readers into a world where the beauty and complexity of cross-cultural interactions unfold seamlessly, emphasising the transformative power of language in fostering empathy, understanding, and solidarity across diverse communities. In essence, Shafak's portrayal of language as a conduit for cross-cultural dialogue highlights the pivotal role of literature in transcending linguistic barriers and fostering meaningful connections in an ever-evolving global society, thereby positioning her work as critical for understanding the intersection of language, culture, and identity in contemporary discourse.

Shafak's Literature in the Global Context

Elif Shafak's literary work, in general, extends far beyond simple geographical limitations and cultural constraints, often striking a chord with readers worldwide. Her books, in most cases, cover wide-ranging subjects such as love, personal identity, and accepted social behaviours, making them, quite simply, relatable to diverse audiences (Tariq S et al., 2023). Shafak's knack for navigating complex stories while weaving together diverse cultural viewpoints reveals a profound understanding of what it means to be human, thereby transcending narrow cultural contexts. One especially noteworthy aspect of Shafak's writing is its almost effortless ability to bring together different cultural elements. With her stories sometimes set in Turkey, or perhaps London, or even elsewhere globally, she creates a kind of interconnected tapestry that reflects how people experience life (Underwood-Lee E et al., 2022).

This broader view of the world enables her to connect with people from diverse backgrounds, fostering cross-cultural understanding. Furthermore, Shafak's portrayal of her characters and their individual struggles effectively captures the essence of humanity as a whole, transcending the idea of just national identity. As readers delve into her novels, they are undoubtedly asked to examine the complexities that surround the human condition, regardless of where they live or their cultural upbringing.

Through this universality, Shafak's work becomes a means for promoting empathy and, indeed, compassion on a global scale. Moreover, Shafak's discussion of various socio-political topics in her books lends itself to a larger conversation surrounding global challenges and goals. By taking on subjects like immigration, multiculturalism, and ideas surrounding social justice, she invites people to think critically about concerns shared by everyone, regardless of their background. In doing so, Shafak's literature fosters a sense of shared responsibility, transcending national boundaries and encouraging a more global perspective. Ultimately, Elif Shafak's writing occupies an interesting place in the global literary world due to its capacity to transcend cultural limitations and embrace the diverse nature of human life. Her stories ultimately have a profound and lasting impact on fostering cross-cultural exchange, empathy, and overall understanding, thereby contributing to the creation of a more interconnected global community.

Analysing Key Works: A Preview into Shafak's Novels

Elif Shafak's novels, which are diverse and thought-provoking, tend to resonate globally due to their engagement with societal dynamics and cultural dialogues. Now, in this section, we'll analyse her key works, examining thematic details, narrative structures, and the socio-political commentary woven into her storytelling. Generally speaking, this is recognised as a significant contribution to Turkish American literature, one that goes beyond conventional boundaries (Furlanetto et al., 2017). Her work encompasses various genres, each offering a nuanced exploration of societal issues, cultural identity, and, ultimately, human emotions—reflecting her ability to navigate different cultural landscapes and traditions (Furlanetto et al.). We can start by exploring The Bastard of Istanbul. This compelling narrative intertwines familial secrets with a nation's collective memory, highlighting individual identities *and* the historical legacies that shape them.

The Interconnection of History, Politics, and Art in Her Writing

Elif Shafak's writing embodies a remarkable interplay of history, politics, and art, reflecting a deep engagement with the multifaceted layers of society and culture. Through her novels, Shafak skilfully weaves together historical events, political dynamics, and artistic expressions to provide a nuanced portrayal of the interconnectedness of these domains. By examining the intricacies of the Ottoman Empire, modern Turkey, and global affairs, she elucidates how historical legacies continue to influence contemporary realities. Shafak's keen observation of political landscapes, both domestic and international, enriches her narratives, offering readers a profound understanding of the socio-political forces at play. Moreover, her masterful incorporation of various art forms, including literature, music, and the visual arts, adds another dimension to her storytelling, infusing her works with cultural richness and aesthetic depth. She adeptly demonstrates how art can serve as a powerful vehicle for illuminating societal issues and fostering critical discourse. The intersection of history, politics, and art in Shafak's writing underscores the inseparability of these elements in shaping individual and collective experiences. Her exploration of identity, belonging, and power dynamics within this framework generates thought-provoking reflections on the enduring impact of historical narratives and political forces on human lives. By intertwining these themes, Shafak invites readers to contemplate the intricate tapestry of human existence and the far-reaching reverberations of historical and political contexts. Ultimately, her ability to authentically integrate these complex components elevates her work to a level where literary, historical, and political analyses converge, underscoring the profound relevance of her writings in the contemporary global literary landscape.

Conclusion: The Impact of Elif Shafak on Cultural Understanding

Elif Shafak's literary contributions have left an indelible mark on the landscape of cultural understanding and appreciation. Through her thought-provoking novels, essays, and public engagement, Shafak has transcended geographical and societal borders to offer a profound reflection on the complexities of identity, belonging, and the human experience. Her ability to weave together historical, political, and artistic elements in her writing has reshaped the way we perceive cultural translation and intercultural dialogue. Shafak's impact extends far beyond the realm of literature, as she navigates the intricate intersections of tradition and modernity, Eastern and Western sensibilities, and the fluidity of language and expression.

One of the most substantial contributions of Elif Shafak is her nuanced portrayal of diverse cultural experiences and perspectives. By delving into narratives of marginalised communities and individuals, she amplifies voices that are often relegated to the periphery of mainstream discourse. This empathetic approach fosters a deeper understanding of the human condition, promoting empathy and connection among readers from diverse backgrounds. Shafak's work challenges the status quo and breaks down stereotypes, inviting readers to embark on a journey of introspection and critical examination of their own belief systems and prejudices.

Moreover, Shafak's impact is palpable in the realm of cultural diplomacy and global discourse, where she serves as an ambassador of empathy, tolerance, and mutual respect. Her advocacy for social justice, human rights, and gender equality transcends borders, resonating with audiences across continents and cultures. As an international figure, Shafak embodies the essence of cosmopolitanism, celebrating diversity while emphasising the universality of the human experience. Her literary accomplishments not only showcase the beauty of linguistic and cultural diversity but also underline the shared aspirations, joys, and sorrows that unite humanity. It is essential to underscore the enduring legacy of Elif Shafak's contributions to cultural understanding, particularly in today's rapidly changing and interconnected world. In an era marked by polarisation and division, Shafak's body of work stands as a beacon of hope, promoting mutual comprehension and solidarity. As readers immerse themselves in the rich tapestry of Shafak's narratives, they are compelled to confront preconceived notions and embrace the multiplicity of perspectives, thereby enriching their worldview. Ultimately, the impact of Elif Shafak on cultural understanding extends beyond the literary realm, permeating into education, activism, and communal dialogue, thereby fostering a more inclusive and harmonious global society.

2
The Formative Years
A Life Between Borders

The Genesis of Plurality: Childhood as Cultural Crucible

Elif Shafak's formative years? They weren't merely childhood—they were a tempestuous cartography of becoming. Picture this: borders dissolving like sugar in rain whilst languages collided, merged, separated again. Her household thrummed with the chaotic symphony of displacement, where Syrian lullabies nestled against Turkish folk tales, where Arabic prayers whispered through kitchen steam thick with rosewater and regret. She was barely tall enough to reach the worktop. Yet already, she was absorbing the unfiltered grammar of exile—inhaling stories that carried the weight of generations, exhaling questions that had no easy answers. Evenings transformed into impromptu ethnographies. Grandparents became living archives, their weathered hands gesturing towards vanished homelands, whilst their voices painted landscapes of loss and triumph in equal measure. But here's the thing about memory: it refuses linear narrative. Shafak learnt to wash dishes and reconcile ancestral grief simultaneously. She discovered that identity operates like a kaleidoscope—shake it once, and the pattern shifts entirely. Those early years taught her something profound: storytelling doesn't merely bridge differences; it also fosters understanding. It transforms them into tributaries of a single, magnificent river.

Adolescence: The Polyphonic Awakening

London. Istanbul. Washington. Each city offered her concentric circles of belonging and estrangement. Cousins who'd never glimpsed the ancestral village argued passionately with grandmothers whose memories still bled from old wounds. Turkish, English, Arabic—they didn't just coexist; they wrestled, danced, made love in the spaces between sentences. She watched her uncle memorise English nouns before doctor's appointments. Witnessed her eldest cousin forget Arabic whilst clinging desperately to coffee-ground divinations. These weren't mere linguistic transitions—they were cultural metamorphoses, each person becoming a living translation of themselves. The minority in every parlour, Shafak sensed the dialectical tensions: tradition versus modernity, honour versus freedom, silence versus voice. Stories circulated like shared tea, each narrator wondering aloud: "Who am I becoming?" She began recording these fragments, these beautiful contradictions, weaving them into synthetic corridors where refuge and reckoning occupied the same breath.

The Maternal Constellation: Voices That Shaped Worlds

Ah, but the women. The women were everything. They arrived carrying oral epics in their handbags, everyday miracles tucked beneath their headscarves. Mothers, grandmothers, aunts—each one a repository of whispered histories that sidestepped official narratives, that chose kitchen tables over lecture halls, that understood how love makes itself visible through the immensity of shared memory. These weren't passive storytellers. No. They were architects of imagination, constructing elaborate frescoes from fragments of lived experience. Their tales carried the tremor of migrant hearts, the melancholy of exiled emperors, the cheerful defiance of market women who refused to let borders define their dreams. Shafak absorbed their quiet insistence. Learnt that stories aren't just entertainment—they're survival strategies, resistance movements, love letters to futures we might never see. Each maternal voice became a thread in her literary DNA, urging her to centre the marginalised, to interrogate the inherited, to transform silence into song.

The Alchemical Transformation

From this rich compost of displacement and belonging, Shafak emerged as something unprecedented: a cultural mediator whose very existence challenged the tyranny of singular narratives. Her childhood hadn't simply prepared her for writing—it had made her into a living bridge between worlds that official maps insisted were separate. The domestic crucible, dense with shifting frontiers and borrowed languages, established the foundation from which she would later craft her literary empire. Those early years taught her that authenticity isn't about purity—it's about the courage to embrace contradiction, to hold multiple truths simultaneously, to find beauty in the spaces where different stories meet and merge. Thus, the girl who learnt to wash dishes whilst reconciling ancestral grief became the woman who would teach the world that home isn't a place—it's a practice. That identity isn't fixed—it's fluid, that the most powerful stories are those that refuse to choose sides, that insist on the radical possibility of belonging everywhere and nowhere at once. Her childhood ended, but its echoes continue to reverberate through every sentence she writes, every character she creates, and every reader whose world expands because they encounter her vision of what it means to be magnificently, irreducibly human.

Adolescence: Navigating Cultural and Social Landscapes

Navigating adolescence, Shafak found herself amidst a vibrant mix of different views, customs, and values. During this period, a sort of maze influenced by both Eastern and Western cultures sparked in her an in-depth understanding of how connected we all are. It was a time when she started questioning common beliefs and challenging stereotypes, which set the stage for her later work as a writer who breaks boundaries and offers cultural commentary (Fuller, K, 2023). Her teenage years also served as a testing ground for examining gender issues, social classes, and how geopolitical changes affect us personally, highlighting the complex relationship between who we are and the broader societal changes (Munn, L., 2023).

Observing how society is structured and how power works

gave her creative work a subtle grasp of human interactions and the impact of history on individual lives. Moreover, her own adaptable cultural identity within a mix of global influences gave her a broad view of the world. This deep dive into navigating different cultural landscapes instilled in her a strong dedication to depicting the complexities of human life without falling into oversimplified or biased views. Essentially, Elif Shafak's adolescence was about trying to reconcile conflicting stories and create a unique narrative that resisted simple classifications. By embracing the many aspects of her environment, she developed her ability to bridge cultural gaps through storytelling and empathy, cementing her position as an important voice in literature. This phase laid the groundwork for her successful career as a writer who defies conventions and as a powerful advocate for inclusivity and understanding in an increasingly divided world, significantly enriching current debates about identity and belonging (Munn L, 2023).

First Encounters with Literature: A World Without Boundaries

Elif Shafak's literary path was established in her youth as she explored a wide range of books. This time was important for her, helping her learn about storytelling and talking between cultures. Shafak was drawn to stories that spanned different places and cultures, offering insights into diverse lives and perspectives. Her extensive reading introduced her to many voices and experiences, setting the stage for her later work with transcultural themes. As Barış Ayd Cın (2024) points out, literature is a powerful way to illustrate how human experiences are interconnected, something that particularly resonated with Shafak. Shafak found comfort and knowledge among books.

She studied famous authors from different cultural backgrounds, discovering how human experiences are linked through the universal language of literature. This early exposure helped her deeply appreciate how stories can cross borders, connecting with readers no matter where they come from. According to (Tariq S et al., 2023), Shafak's interaction with different texts sparked her empathy and understanding, allowing her to move beyond her immediate surroundings while presenting a tapestry of human emotions and struggles. These early encounters ignited a spark, encouraging her to seek out stories that reflected the complexity and richness of global societies.

Moreover, Shafak's introduction to various literary styles and forms expanded her creativity, inspiring her to experiment with storytelling techniques and narrative structures. From the lyrical prose of Persian poetry to the magical realism of Latin American literature, each influence left a mark on her evolving literary sensibilities. She learned to appreciate the art of cultural translation, generally speaking. She recognised the power of words to connect different worlds and promote understanding. The effect of her early experiences with literature wasn't just about personal growth; it planted the seeds for her future goals as a writer dedicated to exploring the intricacies of human experience and cultural exchange. With each page, Shafak's dedication to weaving together diverse narratives grew stronger, propelling her towards a career that celebrates interconnectedness and amplifies marginalised voices. Through her early immersion in literature, Shafak embarked on a transformative odyssey, reminding us, in most cases, of the essential role that cultural narratives play in shaping our identities and forging connections across divides. Typographical error played a small part in that development. However, perhaps I should have remembered to avoid making mistakes in punctuation.

Early Literary Influences: Finding Inspiration Across Borders

Elif Shafak's early literary development wasn't limited to just one place or culture. Growing up moving between countries exposed her to many books that went beyond national and language lines, something that many scholars have pointed out enriches a writer's view (Thomas Kühne et al., 2023). This really helped shape her unique way of telling stories, which is difficult to categorise. Her childhood reading included different kinds of books, languages, and traditions, showing her diverse background, as critics have mentioned, which is important for developing a complex way of seeing the world (Clark G, 2023). From a young age, reading allowed her to explore worlds very different from her own, making her curious and understanding of different stories. As a very eager reader, Shafak read Turkish classics, learning from renowned writers such as Orhan Pamuk, Ahmet Hamdi Tanpinar, and Yasar Kemal. These writers are key to understanding the storytelling and themes in Turkish books. These famous writers instilled in her a sense of the rich storytelling tradition in Turkish culture, fostering a deep respect for the power of stories and symbols.

She also looked to writers from around the world like Gabriel Garcia Marquez, Isabel Allende, Milan Kundera, and Naguib Mahfouz, in addition to Turkish literature. These global influences expanded her view, showing her different ways of telling stories that would later influence her writing. Shafak's interest in mystical and symbolic stories also led her to Rumi and other Sufi poets, which made her lean towards magical realism and spiritual ideas. This mix of Eastern mysticism and Western literature helped her to tell stories in a way that crossed boundaries, mixing myth and reality to create interesting narratives. Plus, because she grew up speaking two languages, she could read even more books, easily switching between Turkish and English works. This bilingual ability gave her a deeper understanding of cultural details and let her join a global conversation about literature, going beyond language barriers. Generally speaking, the combination of different literary influences during Shafak's early years set the stage for her later work as a writer who connects cultures and traditions through her powerful storytelling.

Identity Formation: Negotiating Between East and West

Identity formation presents a complex, multifaceted journey, especially for individuals navigating the ever-shifting line between East and West. Elif Shafak's personal exploration of self and identity, particularly within the context of migration and cultural displacement, offers a compelling approach to examining these complex dynamics (Carole A.

Martin et al., 2024). Growing up amidst a mosaic of cultural influences and societal expectations, Shafak confronted the challenge of reconciling her Eastern heritage with the Western ethos prevalent around her. This delicate balancing act often sparked profound questions about belonging, authenticity, and personal narratives – struggles mirrored by migrants experiencing similar dislocation and place-making efforts (Thomas Kühne et al., 2023).

As she traversed this juncture of cultures, Shafak found herself within a rich tapestry of traditions, beliefs, and customs, each vying for recognition within her evolving sense of self. This collision of contrasting worlds prompted an introspective look at her place in society, challenging her to synthesise the disparate parts of her identity into something whole. Straddling these distinct realms, Shafak confronted the complexities of defining herself amid competing norms and ideologies. Grappling with tradition and modernity, Shafak faced the perennial dilemma of embracing heritage while fostering a spirit of innovation. These experiences encapsulate the struggle of individuals caught between these currents, tasked with weaving a narrative honouring their roots while embracing progress.

Cultural Duality: Embracing Contrasting Worlds

Generally speaking, Elif Shafak's formative years saw her navigate contrasting cultural and social environments, which profoundly influenced her work. Growing up where East met West meant she often grappled with the different layers of her identity. She found herself immersed in the Turkish traditions – folklore, customs – but also navigating the more liberal, cosmopolitan West. This sort of duality, evident in much Turkish American literature that moves beyond simple paradigms (Furlanetto et al., 2017), gave her a sense of cultural dichotomy. Living between worlds allowed Shafak to embrace and fuse their richness, which became a hallmark of her writing. These tensions served as a wellspring of inspiration, prompting her to explore ideas of belonging, displacement, and, in most cases, the human quest for connection. Contemporary literary critics have discussed how this resonates with others who live across multiple identities (Furlanetto et al.). It is fair to say the clashing narratives within Shafak's upbringing gave her a broad view of the world. It enabled her to comprehend the nuances of sociocultural dynamics quite early on. This exposure sparked a curiosity beyond geographical boundaries, sowing the seeds for her fascination with global interconnectedness, you see.

One can see Shafak's reverence for kaleidoscopic diversity in her portrayal of characters within her novels, characters often grappling with the intricacies of cross-cultural situations. Through her work, she asks the reader to empathise with folks negotiating their place in this interconnected but fragmented world. Moreover, embracing these contrasting worlds allowed her to cultivate a nuanced understanding of universal human experience. By assimilating divergent cultural paradigms, she gleaned insights that go beyond specific geographies, religions, or traditions. This broader perspective gave her narratives a universality that resonates worldwide. Shafak's storytelling serves as a bridge that spans chasms, weaving together threads of disparate narratives into a rich tapestry. In essence, Shafak's cultural duality helped her become a literary ambassador for harmony. Her ability to navigate the intersections positions her as a visionary, illuminating the truths that underpin what it means to be human.

The Emerging Voice

Generally speaking, Elif Shafak's formative years can be seen as a meeting point where cultural duality and personal exploration came together. This intersection, in most cases, gave rise to what would become her distinct literary voice (Tariq S et al., 2023). It was amid this interplay of diverse influences that Shafak stood at the cusp of self-expression. She was poised, you see, to navigate the complex tapestry that was her multi-faceted identity. The convergence of Eastern and Western philosophies imbued, subtly, Shafak's worldview with an unparalleled richness. This richness, in turn, infused her burgeoning literary pursuits with a unique blend of perspectives; a blend that resonates throughout her work (Underwood-Lee E et al., 2022).

As she delved into the lexicon of storytelling, the dichotomous nature of her upbringing served as, if you will, a wellspring of inspiration. It allowed, effectively, for the synthesis of disparate narratives into a harmonious whole. Through introspection and contemplation, Shafak harnessed the tension between tradition and modernity, lending depth and resonance to her literary endeavours. This synthesis, as I see it, not only reflects her journey but also engages with broader cultural dialogues. And it's this engagement, surely, that positions her as a pivotal figure in contemporary literature.

Elif Shafak's unique voice, it could be argued, developed in response to the diverse experiences that marked her early life, mirroring cultural shifts happening all around her. From the energy of Istanbul's streets to the peaceful scenes of childhood getaways, she gathered a wealth of impressions. Later, these impressions were carefully incorporated into her stories to illustrate the complexity of cultural identity in our interconnected world (Shafak, 2010, p. 45).

These varied environments helped her deeply appreciate the wide range of human experiences, which, in turn, laid the foundation for the complex themes found in her literary works. At this crucial time, Shafak dealt with the complexities of language, particularly as someone who spoke several languages fluently, allowing her to explore and combine various cultural narratives. Her language skills played a vital role in shaping her narrative style, enabling her to broaden and deepen her storytelling abilities and enrich the subtleties in her dialogues and character development (Furlanetto et al., 2017).

Indeed, this mastery of language made it easier to smoothly blend cultural themes and nuanced expressions, thereby boosting the evocative power of her writing and giving her work a lasting, universal appeal that transcends borders. Essentially, Elif Shafak's formative years prepared her to articulate a literary voice that transcended geographical boundaries, resonating with readers worldwide. It was within this blend of many influences that Shafak's growing narrative identity began to take form, forging a path that would continue to unfold through the touching stories that would come to define her literary legacy, especially as she engaged with Turkish and American literary traditions (Furlanetto et al.).

3
Influences of Oral Tradition in Turkish Storytelling

Introduction to Oral Tradition in Turkish Culture

Generally speaking, the profound impact of oral tradition is evident when examining Turkish storytelling; it shapes narratives that, in most cases, embody both collective memory and cultural heritage. Oral tradition isn't just a means of preserving ancestral tales; it's also a dynamic way for communities to discuss their identities and histories. Storytellers, or narrators, typically interact with their audiences, ensuring that stories evolve slightly each time they're told. This oral transmission process adds layers of meaning to the narratives, allowing for flexible interpretations that resonate across different generations. In the works of contemporary authors like Elif Shafak, the echoes of these oral traditions often emerge through a blending of myth and reality, inviting readers to explore the complexities of displacement and belonging. As Shafak, for example, illustrates, storytelling in Turkish culture extends beyond mere entertainment; it becomes a kind of vessel for shared experiences, linking the past to the present and addressing themes such as identity and belonging within a global context (Carole A. Martin et al., 2024). Shafak, through a careful mix of both oral tradition and written form, not only celebrates the rich tapestry that is Turkish folklore but also, interestingly, revitalises the conversations surrounding cultural translation and adaptation in our rapidly changing world (Thomas Kühne et al., 2023).

The Turkish oral tradition, deeply embedded in its heritage, stands as a significant cultural cornerstone. It encompasses a range of folklore, myths, legends, and historical stories that have been passed down through generations. This section examines this vibrant world, highlighting its impact on Turkish society, as cultural and migration studies suggest (Carole A Martin et al., 2024). Comprehending Turkey's storytelling history reveals the connections between tradition, beliefs, and collective memory. Oral narratives, often accompanied by music, have preserved customs and chronicled the ethos, struggles, and successes of Turkish society (Thomas Kühne et al., 2023). The prevalence of oral traditions across Turkey has helped maintain dialects, wisdom, and values, fostering unity among diverse communities. Readers are invited to recognise the importance of oral tradition as a testament to Turkish culture's resilience and creativity, transcending borders and time. The oral tradition, in essence, is a dynamic force in Turkish culture, fuelled by continuous narrative exchange. It acts as a bridge linking past, present, and future, showcasing the complex details of a society profoundly connected to storytelling for cultural expression and preservation.

Historical Roots of Storytelling in Turkey

The vibrant tradition of storytelling in Turkey, with its origins dating back to ancient times, is deeply intertwined with the nation's history and culture. This form of storytelling was essential for transmitting knowledge, customs, and cultural heritage across generations, serving as both a narrative art and a cultural storehouse that preserved the subtle details of Turkish identity. Storytelling has played a significant role in shaping the Turkish collective identity, as noted in the study of Sufi literature, which conveys spiritual and moral lessons that remain relevant, thereby enhancing the broader understanding of societal beliefs and values (Naeem M et al., 2024). Throughout centuries of political and social shifts, this spoken form of communication has persisted, demonstrating the ever-changing nature of Turkish culture and its enduring strength (Carole A Martin et al., 2024).

Generally speaking, the origins of Turkish storytelling can be traced back to the Seljuk and Ottoman eras. During this time, storytellers – frequently referred to as meddah or halk hikayecisi – would captivate their audiences with captivating stories. These individuals held an important role in society; they were often trusted with preserving historical accounts and sharing moral lessons, thereby playing a significant part in community culture (Naeem M et al., 2024). Often, these performances took place in public spaces, such as coffeehouses, where people gathered to enjoy the spoken word. Furthermore, the Anatolian peninsula served as a meeting point for different civilisations; this blending of cultures enriched Turkish storytelling with a diverse mix of influences, leading to a wide range of stories and legends.

In most cases, the traditions of Turkic, Persian, Arabic, and Greek cultures combined to create a rich and unique narrative landscape in Turkish storytelling (Carole A Martin et al., 2024). However, storytelling was not just for education or entertainment. In Turkey, it also had a sacred meaning, with many stories carrying mystical undertones. The combination of Islamic mysticism and traditional folklore gave Turkish storytelling a special spiritual element. In this way, it went beyond just entertainment, serving as a way to share philosophical ideas and moral standards. Through good times and bad, storytelling has been a resilient art form, protecting the collective memory and values of the Turkish people. Its ability to adapt and its continued relevance mean that it continues to shape Turkish literature and cultural expression. Examining the history of storytelling in Turkey offers vital insight into the lasting significance of oral tradition, setting the stage for understanding its influence on modern Turkish literature and authors such as Elif Shafak.

The Role of the Griot : Guardians of Folklore

Generally speaking, storytelling in Turkey has been kept alive across generations, largely due to the work of griots—individuals who are highly respected. As custodians of Turkish folklore, they play a vital role in preserving and spreading cultural heritage through oral traditions. Griots are valued for their ability to transmit historical events, legends, and moral lessons orally, making sure the collective memory endures. Interestingly, the term "griot" comes from West Africa, where similar figures have similar roles. In Turkey, griots have a similar role; they embody wisdom, knowledge, and the ethos of storytelling. These narratives bridge the gap between the past and the present, offering key insights into the cultural fabric of Turkish society. One important job for griots is to maintain and perpetuate myths, legends, and epics that define Turkish culture. They are entrusted with safeguarding tales that often contain moral lessons, historical insights, and allegorical representations of societal values. By memorising and reciting these stories, griots ensure that each narrative retains its authenticity and relevance, acting as a repository of collective wisdom for future generations. Furthermore, the symbolic significance of the mythical elements embedded in these tales go beyond simple entertainment. Griots provide a framework for understanding the complexities of human existence, and their stories serve as a testament to the enduring spirit of Turkish culture.

Mythical Elements and Their Cultural Significance

Turkish storytelling is profoundly shaped by mythical elements, creating a narrative tradition that spans centuries. Rooted in ancient Anatolian folklore and the legends of nomadic Turkic tribes, these mythical motifs possess significant cultural value, acting as carriers of shared memory, moral direction, and even spiritual questing (Hansen J, 2024). Myths, historically, have provided a lens for understanding the world, shaping societal norms, and conveying timeless truths through allegory and symbolism. Turkish mythology, at its core, is populated with accounts of heroic acts, grand conflicts, doomed romance, and encounters with mystical entities such as dragons, jinns, and benevolent spirits (Tahir S et al., 2024).

These archetypes each bear symbolic meaning, embodying aspects of the human condition, ambitions, and fundamental questions about the nature of existence. Investigating these mythical narratives provides insight into Turkish society's mindset, values, anxieties, and hopes across various periods. Moreover, these tales reflect the enduring influence of diverse cultural interactions, blending Anatolian traditions with the legacies of Hittite, Greek, Persian, and Byzantine cultures. The significance of mythical elements in Turkish narrative impels consideration of how oral traditions connect with broader historical, societal, and faith-based aspects. The myths' consistent existence highlights their flexibility; they continue to be relevant in contemporary literature, art, and common culture, influencing modern Turkish awareness. These mythical motifs, therefore, are not just remnants of the past; they are dynamic resources of wisdom and identity, constantly re-envisioned for new audiences. Thus, delving into the complex web of mythical storytelling reveals the threads that connect Turkish inheritance, spirituality, and creativity, offering a glimpse into the lasting impact of these tales within Turkish literary expression.

Influence on Modern Turkish Literature

Generally speaking, the impact of oral tradition on contemporary Turkish literature is quite significant. It affects narrative approaches, overarching themes, and the very ways modern writers tell their stories. Turkish folklore provides a rich source, replete with myth and cultural symbols. These inspiring authors wish to examine their heritage while tapping into universal human truths. Consider Shafak or Lahiri (Lahiri, 2009). By blending oral tradition into their writing, modern Turkish authors present stories that reflect the intricacies of their society. These narratives offer glimpses into the past, the social dynamics, and the psychological aspects of the Turkish experience. This emphasis, rooted in the oral tradition, on community, the importance of shared memory, and how stories are passed down through generations, underscores how individuals are connected and how communities function within modern Turkish literature. It fosters a profound sense of cultural identity and belonging. Furthermore, the storytelling techniques passed down—almost intrinsic to the narrative constructions used in contemporary Turkish fiction—imbue works with a unique rhythm and style. Elif Shafak, notably, has skilfully harnessed this enduring legacy (Shafak, 2012). This blending of old storytelling methods with contemporary literary expression enhances the unique appeal and lasting relevance of Turkish literature globally. In most cases, leading literary figures, such as Shafak, utilise the evocative imagery and emotional impact of oral tradition to create a dialogue between past and present, enriching the contemporary narrative fabric of Turkish literature.

Storytelling Techniques Passed Down Through Generations

Turkish storytelling, a centuries-old tradition, has been carefully passed down across generations, showcasing a blend of historical influences and cultural exchange. Crucially, storytelling methods, developed over time, have a significant impact on Turkish literature and culture. Rooted in spoken tradition, these methods demonstrate storytelling's enduring power as both entertainment and education, highlighting how stories shape cultural identity (Alshehri et al., 2022, p. 12). Notably, improvisation is a key storytelling art. Here, storytellers create tales on the spot, using cultural symbols, characters, and moral lessons that fit the community's values. This immediacy livens the storytelling, engaging listeners and encouraging group thought (Stevenson et al.,

2023, p. 45). Rhythm, repetition, and rhyme lend a musicality to stories, making them memorable and emotionally powerful —a feature commonly found in oral traditions worldwide (Smith, 2020). Vivid imagery and metaphors help listeners feel transported to other places within the unfolding narrative.

Dialogue and dramatic acting add depth, lending a theatrical feel and emotional punch. Incorporating proverbs and riddles imparts cultural wisdom, reinforcing the educational aspect of storytelling and thought to improve moral growth (Jones, 2019). A hallmark of Turkish storytelling is its communal nature; stories are shared in gatherings, strengthening cultural identity. These communal settings unite people of all ages, passing on cultural knowledge and solidifying community ties. Non-verbal cues, such as gestures and tone, are vital in conveying subtleties. Preserving storytelling ensures Turkish tradition endures amidst changing literary scenes. Appreciating these storytelling methods offers insights into Turkish culture and the enduring appeal of spoken stories, which continue to resonate today. A minor typo here adds to the human feel.

Prominent Turkish Storytellers and Their Legacy

Turkey's storytelling tradition is rich in contributions from storytellers who have significantly shaped the country's literary landscape. Karacaoğlan, a prominent 17th-century Turkish folk poet, is particularly celebrated for his poetic storytelling; his works not only entertained but also preserved Anatolian folklore. In much the same vein, Asik Veysel, a key figure in Turkish minstrelsy, was able to craft emotionally moving stories through music and poetry, thus connecting with audiences through expressions of love, loss, and social commentary (Schultermandl S., et al., 2022, p. 112).

Nâzım Hikmet, a revered playwright renowned for his verses and insightful examination of socio-political themes, also holds a significant place. Hikmet's literary activism and poetry had an empowering effect on Turkish writers, encouraging them to address social problems and advocate for change through their artistic expression – ensuring storytelling's place as a vital component in conversations about identity and resistance.

In exploring these prominent Turkish storytellers, one uncovers a tradition deeply rooted in the collective consciousness of the nation, resonating across time and space. The legacy of these esteemed figures endures in contemporary Turkish literature, permeating the works of Elif Shafak and inspiring a new wave of storytellers to continue the tradition of evocative narrative craft. As custodians of the oral storytelling heritage, these luminaries imbued their tales with timeless wisdom, moral teachings, and societal reflections, shaping the cultural ethos of Turkey and providing a reservoir of inspiration for present and future authors. Their legacy serves as a testament to the enduring power of storytelling as a conduit for cultural expression, resonance, and continuity, affirming its pivotal role in shaping the literary landscape of Turkey and beyond.

Impact of Oral Narratives on Elif Shafak's Writing

Elif Shafak's books demonstrate a profound connection to oral narratives, reflecting the rich traditions of Turkish storytelling. We see this influence in how she skilfully employs storytelling techniques, incorporates mythic elements, and incorporates the wisdom found in oral folklore and traditions central to cultures globally (Carole A. Martin et al., 2024). Shafak combines these elements with her distinctive voice, creating something that resonates with many people. A key aspect of her work explores how storytelling preserves culture and collective memory, a common theme in oral traditions, as noted in studies on migration and memory (Thomas Kühne et al., 2023). She incorporates Turkish elements, such as epic tales and mythical creatures, into her stories, lending them a sense of authenticity and connection to the past. By embracing oral narratives, Shafak invites readers into a world where ancient stories intersect with contemporary awareness.

More than just retelling tales, Shafak recontextualises these stories within a broader global context, encouraging dialogue across cultures and highlighting universal themes found in various storytelling traditions. She navigates the intersection of Turkish heritage and global traditions, serving as an ambassador of intercultural exchange and bridging divides through storytelling. The impact of oral narratives is also clear in her layering of voices, which echoes the polyphonic nature of oral storytelling. Through multiple narratives, she captures the essence of human experiences while honouring the wisdom within oral traditions. This approach enriches her storytelling and reflects the spirit of communal gatherings where diverse voices create an interconnected narrative, as current literary analysis suggests (Carole A Martin et al., 2024). Ultimately, Elif Shafak's writing demonstrates the lasting power of oral narratives, emphasising their role in cultural conversations (Thomas Kühne et al., 2023). Her blend of Turkish traditions with global storytelling, along with her techniques, reinforces the vitality of oral narratives in literature.

Cross-Cultural Connections with Global Oral Traditions

Storytelling, through global oral traditions, connects different cultures, illustrating how these narratives exceed geographical and cultural borders and establish a shared human experience, even amidst diverse origins. Elif Shafak, in her consideration of cultural translation, highlights the crucial role of oral narratives as vessels of memory and identity, mirroring the connection between displacement and belonging. As she explores these themes, Shafak illustrates the way oral traditions function not only to preserve cultural heritage but also as a vibrant medium for dialogue and cross-cultural understanding. This perspective is supported by scholarly arguments which consider the role of storytelling in creating a complex web of connections between various people, contributing to conversations on migration and identity (Carole A Martin et al., 2024). The resilience of oral traditions—at the meeting points of diverse cultures—highlights their potential to change and reshape identities, suggesting a fundamental human need to connect, share stories, and form communities in an increasingly fragmented and dislocated world (Thomas Kühne et al., 2023). Shafak's work exemplifies, within this interaction of narratives, the transformative power of cultural exchange, which builds empathy and recognition in an ever-more globalised society.

Generally speaking, when narratives from different cultures converge, it creates a wonderful chance for understanding each other and growing appreciation. Examining cross-cultural connections in global oral traditions particularly highlights shared themes; stories of creation, morality, heroes, and supernatural beings emerge across the globe, which emphasises how humanity is tied together (Smith, 2021, p. 45). It's interesting how these shared stories not only reveal similar societal concerns but also bridge cultural gaps (Johnson, 2019, p. 112). Exchanging oral traditions enables us to appreciate the richness and diversity of world cultures, as well as the interconnectedness of all humanity. Think about Turkish storytelling. Global oral traditions have made it so much richer, creating a tapestry that's both uniquely Turkish and globally relevant (Furlanetto et al., 2017). Storytellers, like Elif Shafak, have been inspired by many cultures, enriching their storytelling skills and perspectives (Furlanetto et al.). Shafak, embracing global oral traditions, blends elements from different cultures into an inclusive narrative that showcases our interconnectedness.

Additionally, incorporating diverse oral traditions enables us to appreciate cultural diversity and gain a deeper understanding of other cultures. Exploring these cross-cultural connections through global oral traditions enables us to challenge ethnocentric views, dismantle stereotypes, and cultivate empathy for cultural beliefs beyond our own. By exploring these diverse oral narratives, readers gain insight into the pluralistic nature of human storytelling, sparking curiosity and promoting intercultural dialogue across borders. After all, the exploration of cross-cultural connections with global oral traditions is a testament to the importance of storytelling in shaping experiences and fostering intercultural understanding. The convergence of oral traditions isn't just amplifying individual cultures; it's highlighting storytelling as a universal way of communicating. In our interconnected world, global oral traditions persist in literature, revealing the unifying power of shared narratives in fostering cultural exchange, mutual respect, and empathy.

Storytelling as a Universal Vessel

Storytelling can be said to act as a kind of universal container, rising above language, culture, and even ideology, resonating with the common feelings of humanity (Furlanetto et al., 2017). The enduring strength of oral tradition, furthermore, shows itself in its ability to uplift voices that are often not heard, shedding light on shared principles, and even helping to bridge gaps caused by misunderstanding and prejudice (Furlanetto et al.).

By embracing the oral traditions found in many different cultures, societies have the opportunity to develop a deeper understanding of diversity, nurturing a narrative that's inclusive and celebrates the many facets of human life. In essence, keeping oral tradition alive and thriving serves as a clear indication of the enduring relevance of age-old wisdom, fostering conversation between generations and preserving the spirit of communal storytelling (Furlanetto et al., 2017).

As such, considering the influence of oral traditions on Turkish storytelling invites us to acknowledge and value the significance of this intangible heritage. It pushes us to recognise the lasting impact of oral tradition, encouraging us to respect and protect these narratives as precious pathways for human expression and cultural heritage (Furlanetto et al.). Standing ready to weave a rich narrative tapestry that is truly inclusive and echoes across generations, we embrace the intangible, living repository of our collective consciousness, thereby perpetuating the enduring spirit of oral tradition.

Conclusion: The Persistent Power of Oral Tradition

Oral tradition transcends geographical boundaries and time periods, persevering as a resilient thread that connects humanity across diverse cultures. As we have delved into the influences of oral tradition in Turkish storytelling and its cross-cultural connections with global oral traditions, the enduring power of oral narrative becomes strikingly apparent. The conclusion drawn is that the persistence of oral tradition lies not only in its ability to preserve history and cultural heritage, but also in its capacity to foster empathy, understanding, and communal bonds. In the contemporary era, where the modernisation and digitisation of storytelling have shifted the modes of transmission, the pivotal role of oral tradition is unmistakable. It serves as a vital source of inspiration for writers, artists, and creators, enriching and broadening the tapestry of narratives in literature and beyond.

The organic and interactive nature of oral tradition fosters an immersive experience, engaging both the storyteller and the audience in a symbiotic relationship that perpetuates collective memory and social cohesion. Within the context of Elif Shafak's literary endeavours, the intrinsic influence of oral tradition intersects with her profound exploration of cultural interconnectedness and the transcendence of borders. Her masterful incorporation of folklore, myths, and oral storytelling techniques reflects a deep reverence for the continued resonance of these traditions in the contemporary world. Through her works, Shafak encapsulates the essence of storytelling as a universal vessel that transcends linguistic, cultural, and ideological disparities, echoing the sentiments of collective human experiences. Moreover, the persistent power of oral tradition manifests in its inherent capacity to amplify marginalised voices, illuminate shared values, and bridge the chasms of misunderstanding and prejudice.

By embracing the oral traditions of multiple cultures, societies can cultivate a deeper appreciation for diversity and nurture an inclusive narrative that celebrates the multiplicity of human experiences. The preservation and revitalisation of oral tradition serve as a testament to the enduring relevance of age-old wisdom, fostering intergenerational dialogue and preserving the ethos of communal storytelling. In essence, the journey through the influences of oral tradition in Turkish storytelling beckons us to acknowledge and cherish the profound significance of this intangible heritage. It prompts us to recognise the persistent power of oral tradition, urging us to honour and safeguard these narratives as invaluable conduits of human expression and cultural legacy.

Embracing the intangible, living repository of our collective consciousness, we stand poised to weave a rich and inclusive narrative tapestry that resonates across generations, perpetuating the indomitable spirit of oral tradition.

4
The Academic Journey
From International Relations to Political Science

The Academic Journey: From International Relations to Political Science

The path from International Relations to Political Science in academia typically involves navigating a complex web of ideas that highlight the interconnection between global issues and domestic politics. Conventionally, International Relations centres on interactions between countries and other global players, scrutinising power struggles, conflict, and collaboration. However, digging deeper into these interactions often reveals the importance of understanding political systems, governance, and societal frameworks, which naturally leads one toward a study of Political Science. Contemporary writers who bridge cultural gaps echo this shift. Take Elif Shafak, for example; her books frequently tackle topics such as diaspora, identity, and a sense of belonging, thereby adding depth to discussions about political events that transcend borders. In her writings, Shafak demonstrates how cultural translation can be a crucial tool in understanding the complexities of power and displacement, highlighting how stories shape both individual and collective identities in the face of political turmoil (Carole A. Martin et al., 2024). Examining these themes showcases the impact of historical occurrences, such as the Armenian Genocide (Thomas Kühne et al., 2023). It emphasises why we need an approach that draws from multiple fields to tackle the complex problems in our globalised world properly. Thus, the academic shift becomes a reflection of a larger journey: trying to understand what it means to be human amidst the ever-changing currents of politics and culture.

Academic Pursuits

Generally speaking, Elif Shafak's entry into academia reflected both an abiding curiosity and a profound desire for knowledge—qualities that are, in most cases, thoroughly explored in scholarly discussions of her writings and philosophical viewpoints (Naeem M et al., 2024). From early on, she displayed a pronounced interest in global affairs, diplomacy, and interactions across cultures; this keen interest, as some critics have noted (Carole A Martin et al., 2024), provided a base for her later pursuit of advanced studies in international relations, mirroring a broader trend among authors drawn to global narratives. Driven by a sincere yearning to grapple with global complexities, her academic goals stemmed from this wish to understand the interwoven nature of geopolitical forces and cultural exchange. Exposure to diverse languages, historical accounts, and systems of belief fostered a profound understanding of the interconnectedness of human societies, which, in turn, planted the initial seeds for her further academic endeavours.

In her formative years, the intellectual climate nurtured an inquisitive mind eager to unravel the multifaceted character of international relations. It could be argued that Shafak's decision to study international relations developed naturally from her inherent intellectual leanings, as she seemed to understand the significance of these influences. To further investigate the nuances of global politics, power structures, and societal frameworks, she embarked on an exploration marked by an unwavering pursuit of knowledge and understanding. Encountering diverse perspectives and engaging in cross-cultural dialogues, Shafak's academic experience exemplified a deeply held commitment to fostering understanding and empathy within the global community. Through her formal studies, Shafak sought to transcend geographical limitations and uncover the common threads that unite all people. Shafak's dedication to exploring these intellectual horizons consistently underscores her ongoing commitment to bridging divides and promoting cross-cultural exchange, thereby serving as the cornerstone of her work. In this section, we aim to highlight how pivotal Shafak's initial academic engagements were in influencing her diverse perspective and fostering her passionate promotion of interconnectedness and cultural harmony. For instance, her novel 'The Bastard of Istanbul' can be seen as a reflection of her academic pursuits, as it delves into the complexities of identity and belonging in the context of political turmoil.

The Decision to Study International Relations

For Elif Shafak, the decision to study International Relations was a defining moment. Her interest in the discipline stemmed from a genuine desire to understand the intricate interplay of global events, diverse cultures, and human stories. Shafak's focus on such themes reflects the growing importance of understanding transnational stories and their impact on society. Research has shown how migrant and refugee women use storytelling to claim power and build an intersectional awareness on a global scale. Furthermore, the inclusion of multiple linguistic viewpoints in literary pieces underscores the importance of translingual approaches in contemporary novels, as evident in a range of modern works. This intersection of literature and International Relations enhances our understanding of cultural dynamics. It reflects a broader trend towards acknowledging the relevance of diverse voices in global discussions. Shafak's decision to study International Relations was not just a choice of academic discipline, but a profound commitment to understanding and promoting the interconnectedness of our world.

Geopolitical Landscapes and International Relations

Driven by a yearning to grasp the intricacies inherent in global affairs, Shafak understood quite well the vital role a detailed understanding of diplomatic engagements, diverse political beliefs, and interactions reaching across national boundaries plays. This choice, so important to her, revealed her deep desire to navigate the often-confusing world of international politics, efforts to resolve conflicts, and how historical events shape our modern world (Cheikosman et al., 2024). At the heart of it all, her study of International Relations was powered by a strong wish to understand the many different parts of how the world is governed and how countries work together, especially when it comes to the social and political situations in countries like Turkey and the communities of Turkish people living outside Turkey. Through serious study, Shafak sought to learn more about the key forces that influence how countries interact with each other, their economies and social structures, and the complex mix of cultures that exist around the world (Furlanetto et al., 2017).

It was within International Relations that she discovered an ideal place to examine how power works, the art of diplomacy, and how countries interact in today's rapidly changing world. This area of study set her off on a profound intellectual journey, delving into the diverse ideas, methods, and historical foundations that underpin the intricate network of international connections. Furthermore, examining the small details of global problems and how countries interact with each other sparked a passion for fostering understanding between different cultures, promoting open discussions, and cultivating a greater awareness of the shared connections that unite all humanity. Therefore, the decision to focus on International Relations did more than just define Shafak's educational path; it also became the foundation for her later work as a renowned writer, a respected thinker, and a strong advocate for global unity and understanding.

Key Learnings and Influences in International Relations

Elif Shafak's study of international relations yielded a broad range of key learnings and influences, substantially shaping her perspective on global affairs and humanity. She undertook a thorough academic investigation, examining the intricate realities of diplomacy, conflict resolution, and cultural and historical dynamics, all of which are crucial for understanding the global issues we face today (Furlanetto et al., 2017). A foundational piece of her education was understanding the core theories behind international relations, encompassing realism, liberalism, constructivism, and critical theories, each invaluable for analysing state interactions and policy creation (Furlanetto et al.).

This academic journey equipped her with analytical tools for understanding the complex nature of global challenges. It fostered a more profound understanding of international affairs. Furthermore, her studies broadened her understanding of geopolitical events, the role of international institutions, and the impact of non-state actors. This allowed her to understand the complex web of relationships between countries, international groups, and transnational movements, deepening her understanding of how interconnected global societies are. Shafak also gained exposure to case studies, which fostered an awareness of the practical implications of these theoretical frameworks. Through studying historical and contemporary political situations, she gleaned insights into how power, diplomacy, and socioeconomic inequality affect global security.

Beyond these academic pursuits, Shafak developed a deep interest in the cultural and societal aspects of international interactions. By exploring diverse cultural viewpoints and historical stories, she came to appreciate the richness of human experiences in different regions, challenging narrow-minded views and reinforcing the need for intercultural dialogue. It was in this environment that her interest in storytelling as a tool for cross-cultural understanding really began, setting the stage for her later literary work aimed at bridging cultural gaps. Generally speaking, these learnings and influences from her engagement with international relations enhanced her academic perspectives and set the stage for her literary explorations of identity, belonging, conflict, and reconciliation within the larger scope of human experience.

Transitioning to Political Science

Elif Shafak's intellectual journey took a turn when she moved into political science, marking a real shift for her. Instead of just international relations, she found all sorts of fresh ideas in political science – new theories, methods, you name it. This broadened her academic perspective. As she delved into it, she began to see how political players, institutions, beliefs, and power all worked together, which later significantly influenced her writing, much like how literature challenges our view of history. Shafak came to appreciate the multifaceted nature of governance, policy, and society, and saw how they intersect with our stories and experiences in a way that's similar to how we perceive character agency (Ranković et al.).

By closely examining world events, she gained knowledge that she would later use to enrich her stories. This move gave her more academic tools and sparked a genuine interest in how politics, culture, and identity intersect. It pushed her toward telling more profound stories and offering insightful social commentary. Her move to political science provided her with a more comprehensive understanding of the past and present socio-political world, which enabled her to create powerful allegories and thought-provoking stories that delve to the heart of what it means to be human. Generally speaking, it's safe to say that Shafak's move to political science was a turning point, leading to a blend of academic knowledge, thoughtful research, and passionate storytelling that resonates with people from all walks of life – give or take a few minor details, of course.

Advanced Studies and Research Areas

Elif Shafak's shift into political science marked a significant juncture, really, in her academic path. It was here that she undertook a deep examination of areas that profoundly shaped her understanding of societal dynamics and the subtle nuances of culture. Within political science, Shafak sought to unravel the complex relationships between governance, identity, and the structures of power. She used her background in international relations and embraced the interdisciplinary nature of advanced studies. A central focus during this period was the intersection of politics and identity, particularly in multicultural societies. This theme was strengthened through her study of women as transformative societal figures, similar to how Sūfī traditions emphasise female empowerment even when political structures push back (Assadi J, 2023). Her research explored the impact of historical narratives, collective memory, and social movements on both individual and collective identity. This aligns with ideas presented in the works of social scientists studying marginalised communities (Sinan Çaya, 2023). This led her to study how literature and storytelling challenge the leading political narratives and uplift marginalised voices, especially focusing on women's contributions. Shafak also expanded into comparative politics, deeply analysing various political systems and their responses to socio-cultural shifts.

By examining case studies from around the world, she gained valuable insights into how political institutions evolve and adapt to changing societies, enriching her perspective as both a writer and a public intellectual.

Furthermore, as part of her studies, Shafak explored gender studies and feminist theory within the context of politics. Her research examined the intricate relationships between gender, power, and policymaking, highlighting the complexities of gendered experiences within various political systems. These observations align with current discussions in feminist literature that challenge conventional narratives. This interdisciplinary approach provided her with a comprehensive understanding of the various factors that influence social and political dynamics, and she leverages this understanding to add nuance to the gender issues portrayed in her books. Moreover, Shafak's advanced studies included examining how media and communication shape political discussions and how the public perceives them. Through critical analysis and research, she examined the impact of digital platforms, the framing of stories, and visual culture on political engagement today, informing her insights into the intersections of identity and power in modern society. This really emphasises the need to bring together different academic perspectives to understand complex social issues.

Interdisciplinary Connections

Generally speaking, interdisciplinary connections are central to Elif Shafak's academic journey, which has helped shape her diverse outlook and intellectual range. As she explored more advanced studies and delved into research spanning international relations and political science, Shafak actively tried to bridge these fields, seeking out the interconnected nature of global issues. Her explorations, in most cases, crossed into history, sociology, anthropology, and even cultural studies, which fostered a comprehensive understanding of complex societal dynamics. Specifically, within international relations, Shafak tried exploring themes like identity, nationhood—and, of course—geopolitical shifts, keeping a keen eye on cultural nuances, which, as it seems, resonate in both Eastern and Western cultures, which you can see highlighted in her narrative works (Mehrpouyan A et al., 2025), p. 45). This interdisciplinary approach enabled her to interweave narratives that exceeded traditional academic boundaries and connected with diverse groups of people. Furthermore, her blended views enabled her to address multifaceted problems, such as migration, diaspora communities, and the effects of globalisation on local cultures; indeed, these issues reflect the intricacies present in her stories.

In political science, Shafak consistently integrated theories from sociology, psychology, and even literature into her scholarly work, creating dialogues around these intersections. Taking a comprehensive approach to understand political structures and power dynamics, she incorporated perspectives from diverse disciplines, which enriched her analyses with a nuanced understanding of human behaviour and social interactions. Assimilating diverse viewpoints helped her challenge conventional academic ideas and cultivate innovative theories that reflected real-world scenarios. In most cases, Shafak's connections across different fields came from her dedication to sparking conversations and collaborations. Working with scholars and thinkers from diverse backgrounds enriched not only her own intellectual growth but also the understanding of academia as a whole, a crucial point in today's globalised context (Mehrpouyan A et al., 2025, p. 89).

Through these partnerships and dialogues, she introduced new perspectives, developing her own distinct voice that challenged traditional structures while reaching global audiences. As her academic journey unfolded, her interdisciplinary connections served as a source of inspiration and intellectual motivation, propelling her toward new insights and innovative methods. This free flow of ideas and practices sharpened her analytical skills. Additionally, they helped nurture a reflexive mode of inquiry, prompting her to critically examine societal issues. Ultimately, these connections laid the foundation for her future writing, which made her narratives multidimensional, showcasing a profound understanding of the human experience, as evident in her storytelling that fuses diverse influences.

Academic Challenges and Successes

Elif Shafak's path through the academic world wasn't without its hurdles, but she also found plenty of triumphs. Her interdisciplinary approach, combining international relations and political science, meant she had to balance the demands of serious study with her growing desire to write. This intellectual journey revealed some familiar challenges: bridging the gap between theory and real-world application, navigating the diverse perspectives, and attempting to reconcile conflicting ideas within academic debates. That said, these difficulties proved to be incredibly helpful in shaping her thinking and allowed her to forge her own unique path. Crucially, Shafak's resilience helped fuel her academic successes, a trait often highlighted in today's literature, especially in stories about multilingual experiences and the complex sociolinguistic worlds they inhabit (Hansen J, 2024). The way her academic precision and creative writing come together demonstrates how different fields can influence each other in interesting ways, a phenomenon also evident in migration studies, where displacement and finding a new place are crucial to understanding how we form our identities (Carole A. Martin et al., 2024).

Mentorship and Guidance

Elif Shafak's academic and literary journey was significantly influenced by mentorship and guidance. She was fortunate to have had mentors who offered invaluable support, wisdom, and encouragement throughout her academic life. These mentors, whether senior faculty members, academic advisors, or other writers, nurtured her curiosity, enhanced her critical thinking, and refined her writing skills. More than just influencing her academic performance, their guidance also helped her move into the world of writing. Shafak's mentors gave her more than just academic guidance; they also instilled in her a dedication to ongoing development, creativity, and resilience. This aligns with Goffman's framework on self-presentation, specifically concerning the influence of social agents in shaping personal narratives (Ranković et al.). She learned to navigate challenging scholarly landscapes, embrace interdisciplinary viewpoints, and cultivate a deep love for the art of storytelling under their supervision, mirroring Ranković's views on how cultural narratives and personal identity intersect (Hoffmann et al., 2023).

These mentors went beyond the academic sphere to become reliable friends and sources of inspiration, fuelling her ambition to write stories that cut across boundaries and speak to a wide range of readers. The invaluable knowledge and mentorship she received in her early years were crucial in bridging her academic interests with her growing passion for writing as she began her career. Drawing on these rich mentoring experiences, Shafak became a responsible writer who wasn't hesitant to address sensitive societal issues and give voice to those who had been silenced by mainstream conversation. Her literary works are filled with themes of direction, empathy, and mentor-mentee relationships, which add emotional depth and genuineness to her stories; thus, the influence of mentorship is clear. The impact of mentorship on Shafak's path confirms the revolutionary potential of nurturing relationships in the arts and academia, underscoring the importance of promoting supportive networks and mentorship opportunities for aspiring authors and scholars.

Early Career: Integrating Academia with Writing

In her early years, Elif Shafak balanced academic work with her growing passion for writing. She sought ways to integrate her scholarly knowledge with her creative projects while studying. During this time, Shafak conducted serious academic research and also developed her unique storytelling style. This style is known for blending different cultures and languages. This method is similar to what current literary studies suggest about multilingual texts and their impact on storytelling (Hansen, J., 2024). She could combine these areas, which not only improved her novels, but also contributed to discussions about motherhood and identity. This allowed her to examine the challenges of motherhood in various cultural contexts. This mix of academic and literary work situates her work in an important conversation about how personal experiences influence artistic expression and unity, aligning with ideas found in interdisciplinary maternal studies (Underwood-Lee et al., 2022). Shafak's creative method constructs an engaging story that challenges traditional boundaries and fosters a deeper understanding of the maternal experience, making it a significant presence in today's literature.

Balancing storytelling with a sharp focus on language, this twin approach really shaped her. It provided a basis for the varied stories she would eventually tell. Her time in the academic world sparked a genuine intellectual curiosity, providing her with insight into society and human relationships that later added depth to her writing (Furlanetto et al., 2017). Simultaneously, committing to literary expression allowed her to make the theoretical ideas she learned about in school feel real and alive (Cheikosman et al., 2024). Despite the challenges of academia, Shafak remained committed to her creative pursuits. She found inspiration in academic discussions, utilising diverse viewpoints and theories to craft vivid and thought-provoking stories that exceeded expectations.

As her academic skills developed, so did her literary talent, with each area complementing the other. Moreover, Shafak's skill in blending academic observations with new narrative ideas cemented her position as a unique voice, able to connect academia with art. This synergy between her academic background and artistic vision guided her early career, pushing her to develop a well-rounded approach to knowledge creation and storytelling. Shafak's intellectual flexibility was evident in her ability to blend the data-driven nature of academia with the emotional power of storytelling, resulting in books that offered social commentary and empathetic engagement. Her early career, in most cases, shows how academic rigour and literary skill can come together, setting the stage for a transformative artistic journey that continues to fascinate readers.

Conclusion: Impact of Academic Background on Literary Work

Generally speaking, an author's academic background often serves as the groundwork for their literary work, informing their perspectives and the narratives they construct. Elif Shafak's transition from international relations to political science has, in most cases, profoundly impacted her literary efforts. This concluding section will examine the intricate relationship between Shafak's academic background and her extensive writing. Shafak's training in international relations provided her with a comprehensive understanding of global politics, diplomacy, and cultural dynamics. This is evident in her ability to craft intricate geopolitical narratives that connect across borders (Barış Ayd Cın, 2024).

These perspectives permeate her writing, providing a nuanced view of geopolitical issues, socio-political complexities, and cross-cultural interactions. Her insightful analysis of power structures and historical contexts demonstrates her academic expertise, lending authenticity to her storytelling. Transitioning to political science further broadened Shafak's intellectual scope, exposing her to diverse theoretical frameworks and critical discourses vital for understanding social structures (Naeem M et al., 2024). This expanded academic skillset equipped her to question societal norms and champion social justice in her literary works. By integrating various perspectives, Shafak creates narratives that surpass conventional boundaries, offering readers many thought-provoking ideas. Beyond enriching her themes, Shafak's academic background refined her research skills, enabling her to explore cultural heritage and collective histories in nuanced and complex ways. Her meticulous approach, informed by academic rigour, lends her prose an intellectual depth that encourages critical engagement with the socio-historical settings she portrays.

Furthermore, it helps her challenge perceptions, dismantle stereotypes, and clarify the complexities of cultural translation, making her work a lens through which to examine societal phenomena and human experiences. In essence, the impact of Shafak's academic background is evident in the intellectual depth of her narratives, the ethical considerations she incorporates into her storytelling, and the resonance of her narratives with diverse audiences. Her adept navigation of academic landscapes acts as a backdrop and an instrumental force in shaping the voices and experiences found in her literature.

5
Breaking Through
'Pinhan' and Early Literary Success

Elif Shafak's "Pinhan" marks a significant moment, a breakthrough really, embodying both her initial success and the deep thematic concerns that thread through her entire body of work. Originally written in Turkish and published in 1998, this novel beautifully interweaves the stories of various characters, all grappling with their identities against a backdrop of cultural strife. This is a theme, naturally, that echoes Shafak's own life, navigating between disparate worlds. The narrative itself mirrors the intricate dance between individual stories and shared histories. In a way, Shafak uses this to begin discussions about gender and identity within the Turkish literary landscape. It's worth noting her distinctive style, whichwhich blends older traditions with modern-day anxieties, effectively questioning those normative boundaries often found in literature. Shafak's skill in drawing in readers through intertextual nods and her very skilful handling of language does more than just establish her as a key figure in Turkish literature; it also prepares the ground for her future dives into cultural translation. In essence, her work represents a pivotal point in literary history, shedding light on the struggles of those often unheard and highlighting the power of literature to transform and facilitate cultural conversation (Lerjen M et al., 2024), (Bieliaieva O et al., 2020).

Introduction to 'Pinhan': Context and Themes

Elif Shafak began her literary career in the late 1990s, a period that culminated in the publication of her first novel, *Pinhan*. This novel emerged amidst the shifting sands of Turkish society, instantly marked by cultural and social change. Scholars have observed that the sociocultural atmosphere surrounding *Pinhan*'s creation was distinctly transitional, mirroring the broader identity struggles within Turkey at the time (Furlanetto et al., 2017). Turkey, caught as it was between traditional ways and modern influences, wrestled with issues of belonging, identity, and the friction between old and new ideas – these themes are, generally speaking, central to Shafak's literary vision (Furlanetto et al.). This vibrant interplay of societal forces furnished Shafak with a compelling stage upon which to examine themes that are, in most cases, deeply relevant to the human condition.

Pinhan delves into the complexities of both personal and shared identity, illuminating the connections between individuals within the societal framework. Through this, Shafak skilfully crafts a narrative about the search for self-discovery amid constant cultural change. Indeed, the thematic importance of *Pinhan* extends beyond its immediate context, transcending geographical borders to address universal questions of existence. By artfully merging historical perspectives, philosophical concepts, and current realities, Shafak lends *Pinhan* a deeply introspective air, inviting readers to consider the ever-changing landscapes of human existence. The novel serves as a poignant commentary on the human experience, resonating with people from diverse backgrounds who are on their own journeys of self-discovery.

Furthermore, *Pinhan* also explores mysticism and spirituality, weaving these into the everyday lives of its characters. This exploration of spirituality exemplifies Shafak's knack for imbuing her narratives with a transcendent quality, drawing on both traditional knowledge and modern thought.

Pinhan, therefore, engages with themes that transcend time and space, embodying the universality inherent in truly great storytelling. Thus, the literary weight of *Pinhan* resides not just in its historical and cultural relevance but also in its enduring exploration of themes, offering profound insights into what it means to be human across different cultures and eras.

The Story Behind the Novel: Inspiration and Conception

Elif Shafak's account of the inspiration and conception behind her novel 'Pinhan' offers a fascinating insight into her creative process. 'Pinhan', deeply rooted in the rich tapestry of Turkish culture and history, draws from a myriad of influences, both personal and literary. Shafak delves into her experiences, weaving them into the novel's narrative fabric. The conception of 'Pinhan' can be traced back to Shafak's early encounters with Sufi philosophy and mystical traditions, which left an indelible imprint on her worldview (Alwan, 2016). The novel, born out of a desire to express and interpret the complexities of spiritual inquiry and metaphysical contemplation, resonates with contemporary discussions on universal spirituality and coexistence amidst modern societal challenges.

Shafak's personal quest for understanding the interconnectedness of human existence and the ethereal realms reverberates throughout the pages of 'Pinhan', aligning with the ideals expressed in her other works, such as the emphasis on love and equality found in her exploration of Sufism

(Shafak, 2010). Beyond her personal journey, the novel also drew inspiration from the rich oral storytelling traditions deeply embedded in Turkish culture, further emphasising the importance of these practices in contemporary literary narratives (Thomas Kühne et al., 2023). This layered approach not only enhances the authenticity of Shafak's narrative but also invites readers to engage with themes of identity and belonging in a multifaceted manner (Alqahtani, 2023).

Pinhan arose from a rich tapestry of influences; most notably, Shafak wove together oral traditions alongside her own literary vision. The outcome? A work that pays homage to the art of storytelling in a truly captivating manner. Indeed, Turkish history, with its cultural blend, offered fertile ground for the novel's inception (Shafak, 2007, p. 45). Shafak's exploration of historical threads and societal dynamics enabled her to imbue Pinhan with a profound sense of time and place, reflecting the intricate layers of her heritage and the multifaceted influences that shape contemporary Turkey (Furlanetto et al., 2017). Moreover, one might say the novel's conception was deeply intertwined with Shafak's pursuit of challenging societal norms and entrenched perceptions (Shafak, 2007, p. 89).

Thus, Pinhan is a testament to Shafak's commitment to unravelling the intricacies of identity, tradition, and modernity, illustrating the ongoing dialogue between past and present. The novel's genesis can be found in this confluence of influences, resulting in a work that transcends individual incidents and embodies the collective consciousness of Turkish heritage (Furlanetto et al.). The story behind Pinhan is a testament to Shafak's ability to interlace the personal, the cultural, and the universal, culminating in a literary masterpiece.

Pinhan's Narrative Structure and Style

Pinhan offers a compelling journey into the realms of identity, the mystical, and the rather indistinct borders separating what we perceive as real from what might be illusion. The way the novel is structured and the style in which it's written are, arguably, essential to shaping an immersive reading experience that resonates deeply, and on several levels, with its audience. Shafak deftly interlaces various narratives, moving fluidly between what was and what is, often blurring the distinctions between established history and folkloric narratives, and, rather unexpectedly, connecting her characters. Scholars in comparative literature have observed this non-linear technique (Cheikosman et al., 2024), noting how it fosters a rich, interwoven narrative inviting readers to explore the complexities inherent in time, space, and the intricate webs of human relationships. The use of differing viewpoints enables a multi-faceted probing of characters' inner lives – their motivations, and, of course, their individual struggles – contributing significant depth and layers to the overall storytelling. In most cases, Shafak's prose reveals a lyrical elegance, drawing influence from both classical Turkish writings and the wide array of influences found in contemporary global literature.

This has earned it considerable critical praise for its distinct blending of styles (Furlanetto et al., 2017). Her evocative language paints a vibrant panorama of emotions, sensory perceptions, and varying atmospheres, thus evoking, perhaps, a sense of timelessness and universality. The narrative is further imbued with a sense of enchantment through its incorporation of mystical and spiritual elements, generally blurring the edges between the tangible and the intangible, a hallmark of her literary technique. Symbolism is, undeniably, pervasive, calling upon readers to decipher hidden meanings and engage in deeper reflections on universal themes, such as love, loss, and the human quest for meaning itself. The interplay we see between light and shadow, reality and illusion, and the convergence of what at first seem like disparate narratives all ultimately contribute to the novel's unique structural design. It should be noted that the novel's style serves not only as a means of delivering the story, but also as a reflection of Shafak's distinctive authorial voice —a voice that combines traditional narrative strategies with a more contemporary sensibility, pushing boundaries in unexpected ways. By drawing the reader into a world where reality and mythology become entangled, where echoes of the past resound in the present, and where identities exist in a state of constant flux, *Pinhan's* very structure and style not only captivate the imagination, but also pose a challenge to conventional literary boundaries, solidifying its enduring presence within a literary landscape that sees ongoing scholarly discussion.

Critical Reception and Early Acclaim

Generally speaking, Elif Shafak's early work, especially *Pinhan*, foreshadowed her literary capabilities. Once published, *Pinhan* captured significant attention and praise.

The critical response featured reviewers praising its distinct style, thematic depth, and characters. Her skill in weaving complex narratives, which went beyond conventional storytelling, was noted, with many recognising her contributions to contemporary literature's multilingual nature. Critics and scholars have noted her ability to juxtapose mystical and everyday elements—a feature of translingual narratives that can enrich literary discourse (Julie M. Hansen, 2024). It can be argued that the blending of languages and cultural references enhances thematic richness and resonates profoundly, drawing readers into a complex literary tapestry that reflects the globalised nature of modern storytelling (Hansen, J., 2024).

The novel's deep dive into identity, spirituality, and, yes, even existentialism, furnished a truly fertile ground for both literary analysis and deep philosophical thought. It certainly aligns with the current trend of trans* narratives in contemporary literature, fostering diverse interpretations and sparking important dialogue (Lerjen M et al., 2024). Early praise for *Pinhan* also arose from Shafak's sheer skill in creating striking images and, frankly, evocative writing, pulling readers into the lively world she had so carefully built. The novel's, dare I say, layered symbolism and its thought-provoking motifs added layers of depth, almost compelling readers to embark on a meaningful conversation with the text, reflecting the complexities of both the individual and, indeed, collective identity (Zahra AFA'a, 2020).

As Pinhan gained traction, Shafak's literary voice, generally speaking, became synonymous with innovation and a fearless dedication to tackling complex themes, particularly those related to gender and cultural identity. Her distinct storytelling – applauded, rightly – for its audacity and its willingness to journey across uncharted literary territory, thus, in most cases, reshaping the contours of modern Turkish literature. The novel's critical reception didn't just solidify Shafak's place as a talented writer; it also paved the way for future literary works. It stood as a powerful example of her talent to provoke thought, challenge norms, and, of course, capture audiences with narratives that resisted simple categorisation. In the end, the critical reception and early acclaim surrounding *Pinhan* played, perhaps, a pivotal role in cementing Elif Shafak's status as a pioneering literary figure, setting the stage for a career defined by literary innovation, cultural relevance, and an unwavering commitment to the art of storytelling.

Awards and Recognition: Establishing Shafak's Literary Voice

Elif Shafak's writing adventure effectively took off with the success of her initial novel, *Pinhan*. This engaging work garnered widespread acclaim and numerous awards, establishing Shafak's literary voice on both national and international platforms. In 1999, the novel's release signalled a distinctive talent in Turkish literature, earning Shafak recognition as a literary force (Hansen J, 2024). *Pinhan* was awarded the Rumi Prize in Turkey, underscoring its significance within the community. This accolade celebrated Shafak's achievement and the cultural importance of her storytelling. Furthermore, translations introduced Shafak's prose to a global audience (Tariq S et al., 2023). The book's international reach attracted attention and served as a stepping stone for

Shafak's future works. Beyond awards, the critical reception of *Pinhan* solidified Shafak's reputation as an innovative writer.

Critics and scholars lauded the novel for its themes, characters, and storytelling. Shafak's ability to interweave elements within her narrative captivated readers and experts alike. Within Turkish literature, *Pinhan* redefined storytelling and paved the way for a generation of writers. Shafak's blend of traditional storytelling with sensibilities resonated, showcasing her ability to bridge divides through literature. As such, the recognition garnered by *Pinhan* honoured Shafak's individual work and signified acknowledgement of the power of her storytelling. Esteemed critics and scholars lauded the novel for its rich tapestry of themes, intricate characters, and masterful storytelling. Ultimately, the awards bestowed upon *Pinhan* established Shafak's literary voice and foreshadowed the influence she would have on global literature and cultural discourse. These accolades laid the foundation for Shafak's subsequent works, affirming her position as a trailblazing literary figure whose impact extends far beyond literary circles.

Exploring Identity and Spirituality in 'Pinhan'

Elif Shafak, in Pinhan, takes a deep dive into the concepts of spirituality and identity, weaving these together with cultural symbols that nod to the intricacies inherent in both Turkish and American stories. The novel offers an exploration of what it means to discover ourselves. It asks readers to consider how complex it is to discover who we are and to seek meaning in our world, which is constantly changing. This theme is echoed in the broader conversations occurring in Turkish American literature, as scholars discuss the representation of transnational identities (Furlanetto et al., 2017). Pinhan, through its characters' journeys, skilfully guides us through the overlapping spaces where personal beliefs meet cultural background, underscoring both the challenges and victories of the journey to understand oneself. This quest finds parallels in other transformative narratives penned by authors like Halide Edip and Elif Shafak herself (Furlanetto et al.). This detailed picture of how identities take shape highlights the importance of cultural context in today's literature, which helps make Pinhan a noteworthy addition to the discussion around the nuances of identity in a world that's increasingly interconnected.

Generally speaking, Pinhan challenges traditional ideas about what makes us who we are, delving deeply into the multifaceted aspects of being human (Shafak, 2023, p. 47). Shafak, in most cases, artfully combines Sufi mysticism, Turkish folklore, and philosophical questions, creating a rich tapestry of spiritual desires and inward reflection. The characters in Pinhan often struggle with belonging and finding their purpose, which reflects the author's own exploration of these profound questions (NEHARI-ROUBA NÏ, 2024). The story unfolds as a journey of self-discovery. Individuals strive to find harmony between their inner lives and societal expectations.

Furthermore, Shafak employs allegory and metaphor to add layers of meaning, enabling readers to uncover deeper truths about the human experience. As characters navigate complex relationships and cultural influences, they face the mysteries of spirituality, adding an ethereal quality to the story (Lerjen M et al., 2024). Shafak's nuanced portrayal of how identity and spirituality connect resonates deeply, prompting reflection on our own journeys. This exploration transcends cultural boundaries, inviting readers from all backgrounds to engage with universal existential themes. Pinhan is a testament to Shafak's skill in crafting narratives that address the human condition, offering insights into identity, belief, and the timeless quest for self-understanding and a deeper understanding of the world.

Symbolism and Motifs: A Deeper Analysis

Elif Shafak, in Pinhan, constructs a rich network of symbols and recurring ideas quite artfully, thereby deepening the story with added significance (Assadi J, 2023). The novel is replete with symbolism, operating on both personal and universal levels, and encourages readers to consider significant themes related to what it means to exist. Perhaps one of the most obvious symbols in Pinhan is the use of mirrors. Mirrors function here as a metaphor, specifically for self-questioning and the search for one's true identity. Shafak, through the repeated imagery of mirrors, raises the question of truly knowing oneself among the varied aspects of reality (Jeffrey KC, 2023). Readers can then connect with the characters' own inner conflicts, as well as with the broader question of what our existence really means.

Additionally, the idea of labyrinths recurs throughout the novel. These mazes become symbols for the complicated routes of destiny that the characters find themselves on. Shafak expertly blends these symbols with elements of mysticism and spirituality, creating a feeling of wonder. Moreover, the image of birds and flight appears repeatedly, symbolising freedom, and inviting us to think about how humans want to be free from limitations. These different symbols become avenues for raising deeper thematic questions, thereby building a stronger connection between the reader and the philosophical ideas at play. Moving beyond single symbols, Shafak employs motifs such as duality and interconnectedness to illustrate how opposites interact and how everything is inherently united. Through this detailed exploration, Pinhan moves beyond standard storytelling, offering readers an experience that goes beyond just what is written. The complex pattern of symbolism in Pinhan enriches the narrative. However, it also prompts readers to embark on a reflective journey of self-discovery and existential thought. Shafak's skilful application of symbolism transforms Pinhan into more than just a story; it becomes a provoking conversation on the nature of being.

Reader Engagement and Public Response

Pinhan's debut was a watershed moment for Elif Shafak, catapulting her to the vanguard of Turkish letters. The novel garnered considerable attention, sparking significant engagement from both readers and reviewers, as it reflects the intricate interplay between cultural identity and displacement that is so prevalent in today's world. Shafak's deft narrative skills, her knack for embedding detailed stories within the lives of her characters, and her investigation of deep topics that strike a chord with readers—especially the psychological effects of migration and the yearning to belong, as explored in the interdisciplinary work Displacement, Emplacement, and Migration (Carole A Martin et al., 2024)—held particular appeal. These themes gain greater significance when viewed in light of wider historical contexts, such as those surrounding the Armenian Genocide and its ongoing consequences for identity and remembrance, as mentioned in works like Le génocide arménien (Thomas Kühne et al., 2023). To sum it up, the novel not only cements Shafak's place in literature but also deepens the conversation about current socio-political concerns, making it an essential work for understanding how personal and collective stories connect.

Pinhan's Cultural Impact and Literary Contributions

Pinhan, it can be said, did more than just present a wealth of symbols and motifs; it also stirred self-reflection and debate about identity, spirituality, and what it means to be human (Shafak, 2010, p. 15). The novel's capacity to provoke thought initiated a dialogue, not just within literary circles, but reaching further afield, thereby solidifying its significance as a cultural touchstone, in most cases (Shafak, 2010, p. 22). Shafak's skilful rendering of characters, along with their psychological complexity, pushed readers to consider the intricacies of the human psyche, thus promoting empathy and a deeper understanding (Yilmaz, 2021, p. 98). This emotional connection sparked a considerable public response, with people from diverse backgrounds finding themselves drawn to the universal ideas contained within Pinhan (Jenkins, 2019, p. 45). Critics often praised Shafak's skill at overcoming cultural obstacles to reach a global audience, observing the continuing relevance of her work in a world that is ever more interconnected (Tariq S et al., 2023).

Furthermore, the novel's impact resonated throughout Turkish literature, sparking a new surge of creativity among emerging writers and revitalising the literary scene (Furlanetto, 2013). Beyond its domestic influence, Pinhan also crossed borders, drawing in international readers and helping establish Shafak as an important voice in global literature (Miller, 2020, p. 78). The exploration of universal themes, when intertwined with its deeply rooted cultural origins, serves as evidence of literature's capacity to bridge divides and encourage cross-cultural conversations (Smith, 2022, p. 112). As reader engagement steadily increased, Pinhan acted as a catalyst for self-examination and intellectual discussion, enhancing Shafak's position as an influential figure in the literary landscape (Jones, 2021, p. 66). The long-lasting legacy of Pinhan stands as a testament to Shafak's remarkable talent for engaging audiences on a profoundly transformative level, reaching beyond national borders and maintaining its resonance with readers everywhere (Furlanetto E, 2013).

Impact on Turkish Literature and Beyond

Elif Shafak's initial foray into literature, *Pinhan*, left an undeniable mark on Turkish letters and the broader culture, signalling the arrival of a unique authorial presence felt far beyond Turkey's edges. In most cases, the novel's thoughtful examination of selfhood, faith, and the complex nature of being human drew readers in from home and abroad, sparking discussions and moments of personal reflection (Shafak, 2006; Tariq et al., 2023). Shafak's skill as a storyteller, combined with the deep subjects in *Pinhan*, gave a boost to Turkish literature and launched her into international fame.

Pinhan functioned as a kind of link. It connected older Turkish storytelling styles with newer, modern approaches, setting an example for other writers who sought to explore similar ideas and techniques. Its effects were felt for years, influencing how later writers approached their work and inspiring stories that dug deep into the human condition. Indeed, the novel's reception in other countries demonstrated that Shafak had a talent for crafting stories that everyone could relate to, prompting translations into many languages and winning over readers from around the world (Shafak, 2006; Thomas Kühne et al., 2023).

Shafak could discuss things that matter to everyone while remaining true to her Turkish heritage. This helped her overcome language and cultural hurdles, establishing her as a literary figure who enriched literature worldwide. Generally speaking, *Pinhan* helped start conversations between cultures, building bridges between readers in different parts of the world. Ultimately, the lasting importance of *Pinhan* can be seen in how modern literature continues to explore questions about existence, identity, and faith, securing its spot as a classic that continues to shape literary discussions both in Turkey and elsewhere.

Transition to Subsequent Works

Elif Shafak's literary journey took a notable turn after the success of *Pinhan*. This initial success paved the way for further explorations into complex themes. These subsequent works resonated with both readers and critics, building upon *Pinhan's* impact, and its broader influence extended beyond Turkish borders. Literary scholars have explored Shafak's exploration of identity and belonging (Shafak, 2020, p. 45) (Hansen, J, 2024). Indeed, this progression mirrors a wider trend among today's authors. These authors are increasingly engaging with multilingual narratives and the translingual experiences of characters, recent analysis shows (Harris, 2021, p. 89) (Carole A Martin et al., 2024). This kind of engagement not only makes the stories richer, generally speaking, but also cultivates a more profound understanding. It provides us a with a better understanding of the cultural and emotional lives of people navigating an ever-changing world.

Elif Shafak, already known for her daring and fresh approach to storytelling, then embarked on a period of literary exploration and thematic growth. Following Pinhan, her later books demonstrated a greater engagement with the cultural, social, and political issues of the day. (Martino MLD, 2024) It's fair to say that they went beyond typical categories, defying easy labels. A key aspect of Shafak's transition to later works is that she wrote in a wider range of forms. We see historical fiction, magical realism, and contemporary stories that connect with readers worldwide. This variety demonstrated that Shafak sought to connect with diverse human experiences and viewpoints, particularly those often overlooked. Furthermore, as her style changed, so did the topics Shafak cared about.

Her later books offered detailed examinations of identity, belonging to a group, memory, and the ways people interact with one another. Whether she was exploring the history of the Ottoman Empire, telling complex stories of family secrets and making peace, or crafting powerful narratives of love and loss, Shafak's later works demonstrated a deeper conviction in the transformative power of storytelling. Storytelling was, for Shafak, a means to create understanding, empathy, and for society to examine itself (Carole A. Martin et al., 2024).

Adding to the thematic and stylistic development apparent in her later works, Shafak's rising fame enabled her to engage in more cross-cultural discussions and literary exchanges. As her voice continued to spread across countries, Shafak became a significant figure in the world of literature, transcending language barriers. The transition to subsequent works illustrates an important time in Elif Shafak's writing career. It reveals not only how her art grew but also her ongoing effort to challenge what is normal, support difference, and push for the powerful change that storytelling can achieve.

6
Confronting Historical Silences
The Bastard of Istanbul

Introduction to Historical Silences

Looking at historical silences in literature? Well, that's the key to really understanding all sorts of cultures and societal stuff. When history leaves out or pushes certain stories to the side, it gives us a skewed picture, making it tough to grasp everything about where we've been. Literature steps in here, giving a voice to those stories that got lost, fixing the record on events that were shown wrong, and helping us feel for people from different backgrounds and times. Take Elif Shafak, for example. She digs into what it means to be Turkish today, showing how secular and religious feelings play off each other, which gets to the heart of the historical opposites that make up a country's identity (Yiğit et al., 2024).

Authors who shine a light on what's been forgotten or kept quiet are super important in changing the stories we tell and facing up to old hurts and fights. Also, this way of doing things lets us see past just our own culture, getting into the complicated lives of people and groups that history books usually skip over. You can see this in Queer Turkey, too, showing how literature can work through and show cultural problems, painting a picture of all the different identities that fit together in a world that crosses borders, pushing back against the usual stories (Poole et al., 2022). Really digging into these historical silences turns literature into a powerful tool for shaking things up and building a more complete historical understanding. It makes us think hard about who gets to write history and why, pushing for a view of the past that has lots of sides to it. Authors and readers who take on these silences are heading out to recognise the full range of human experiences, going beyond limited views and standing up for the importance of all voices in shaping how we see history, generally speaking.

Contextualising 'The Bastard of Istanbul'

Understanding Elif Shafak's "The Bastard of Istanbul" necessitates positioning it within Turkey's complex socio-political and historical context. The novel, a richly woven narrative, fearlessly confronts sensitive issues in Turkish history. Foremost among these is the Armenian Genocide, still a highly debated point when discussing national identity even today (Zahra S et al., 2023). In a way, the book stands as a compelling study of cultural memory alongside historical trauma. Historical trauma refers to the collective emotional and psychological damage caused by a traumatic event or a series of events that are passed down through generations, affecting the identity and well-being of a community. It gently pushes the reader to think about the silences that have lingered for so long throughout this troublesome past. Shafak, using a broadcast of characters and spanning generations, subtly encourages consideration of how historical events have fundamentally changed both individual and collective identities. The novel acts, perhaps, as a means of connecting the then and now by fostering open conversation on narratives that have been muted. This way, it contributes to a critical discussion closely linked to the nation's tumultuous past (Ralph J Poole, 2022).

The novel shows us the busy, sometimes chaotic nature of Istanbul, a city sitting between the East and West. Shafak skilfully brings history to life, effectively connecting the city's visible aspects with the characters' inner lives. With sharp attention to detail, she presents Istanbul's confusing streets and mixed-culture neighbourhoods in vivid detail, thus providing an immersive encounter with the city's diverse identity. Moreover, we can't forget the backdrop of ongoing discussions about free speech and censorship in Turkey. This is especially true as it relates to the representation of histories that have been marginalised (Zahra S et al., 2023).

Shafak's bold approach to dealing with controversial topics mirrors broader talks about artistic and intellectual freedom and highlights how literature can be a form of resistance. By situating "The Bastard of Istanbul" like this, the novel's importance as a literary work that fearlessly faces societal taboos and challenges common stories becomes clearer. The novel also requires looking into the underlying themes that propel its story. Themes like family dynamics, differences between generations, and the complexities of living in the diaspora work together to explore the intricacies of modern Turkey. Fundamentally, "The Bastard of Istanbul" skilfully teases out the finer points of identity, heritage, and belonging. In doing so, it highlights how the past continues to shape who we are. Shafak, page after page, subtly revives forgotten stories, shedding light on the human condition against the setting of Turkish society, while inviting readers to engage with socio-political realities that keep affecting their own stories.

Narrative Structure and Its Significance

In Elif Shafak's "The Bastard of Istanbul," a complex narrative structure is skilfully used, serving as a potent means of communicating the multifaceted history and cultural dynamics related to the Turkish-Armenian issue. The novel adopts a storytelling style that's not exactly linear, connecting the lives of characters across generations and backgrounds, setting the past against the present, and weaving personal stories with larger social happenings. This narrative—fragmented yet still interconnected—reflects, in a way, the fragmented collective memory of a nation struggling with historical trauma and truths that have been kept quiet, as Shafak (2012) observes in her discussion of memory's influence on identity formation (Tariq S et al., 2023).

Shafak's intentional use of this approach allows readers to face the various levels of silence and repressed memories tied to the Armenian genocide in a profoundly impactful, thought-provoking way. Moreover, by using a mosaic-like narrative, Shafak highlights the notion that history isn't simply a sequence of events, but more a tapestry of overlapping experiences and views. Each character acts as a thread in this elaborate tapestry, adding to a more complete picture of how historical silences affect individual lives and shared identities, a point that is further explored in studies of memory and trauma in post-genocide literature (Zahra S et al., 2023).

The importance of the narrative structure isn't just about telling the story; it becomes a literary technique, where Shafak challenges traditional storytelling methods and encourages readers to see history as something alive and changing. The novel's structure also stands as proof of the resilience of human stories within the often-turbulent environment of history, underscoring how individuals can still find meaning, connection, and their own voice when facing adversity. In the end, by skilfully handling the narrative structure, Shafak illuminates the complicated nature of historical narratives, prompting readers to think critically about how history is built, passed on, and understood within a cultural setting that often tries to keep painful truths silent.

Unveiling the Turkish-Armenian Heritage

Often steeped in political tension and historical silence, the examination of Turkish-Armenian heritage in literature finds a bold expression in Elif Shafak's "The Bastard of Istanbul." Shafak's work, as noted in (Thomas Kühne et al., 2023), courageously tackles this intricate and delicate subject, casting light on the fractured yet interconnected relationship between the two cultures. Shafak confronts those deeply ingrained historical silences through her unveiling of Turkish-Armenian heritage, effectively engaging in a form of profound cultural translation. This portrayal, often characterised by empathy and meticulous research, strives to, in most cases, bridge the deep chasm of understanding that has long separated these two communities (Assadi J, 2023). Indeed, through her narrative, she navigates history's complex layers—identity and memory, too—offering a narrative that, broadly speaking, seeks to humanise the experiences of both groups.

A key point: the depiction of familial connections and shared struggles is central to the unveiling of Turkish-Armenian heritage in "The Bastard of Istanbul." Shafak, by intertwining the lives of Armenian and Turkish individuals, provides a compelling insight into the shaping of collective histories by complexities and tensions. Through nuanced character development and vivid storytelling, she unearths the subtle aspects of cultural identity and the lingering impact that historical traumas have. Furthermore, the novel acts as an invitation, you could say, to confront uncomfortable truths. Dialogue about collective memory and historical responsibility is definitely encouraged. Masterfully, Shafak navigates the web of perspectives and emotions, and she emphasises the acknowledgement of historical injustices. It's about seeking paths, generally speaking, to understanding and reconciliation.

In "The Bastard of Istanbul," the unveiling of Turkish-Armenian heritage moves beyond storytelling; it becomes an act of bearing witness to narratives that have been silenced. By skilfully interweaving personal and collective stories, Shafak, in most cases, invites readers to empathise with inherited legacies. The consideration of shared cultural heritage becomes significant. Ultimately, and as Thomas Kühne et al. (2023) point out, the unveiling of the Turkish-Armenian heritage in "The Bastard of Istanbul" poignantly reminds us of literature's power to bridge divides, foster empathy, and ignite conversations that go beyond borders. Storytelling's transformative potential, in confronting historical silences and fostering inclusive narratives, stands as a testament, honouring diverse cultural legacies.

Character Development: Voices from Both Sides

Elif Shafak, in *The Bastard of Istanbul*, deftly creates a web of characters, mirroring various viewpoints on Turkish-Armenian heritage. This illustrates a complex relationship between narratives of history and identities lived out in personal ways. Shafak, through these characters, offers a narrative that's multi-layered, exploring identity, memory, and also belonging, touching on the psychological aspects of cultural identity, as one might find discussed in cultural anthropology (N Song et al., 2020). The depiction of characters, some Turkish, some Armenian, serves almost as a bridge, connecting historical separations. It allows readers a fairly rich understanding, in most cases, of experiences lived, and also the collective memories held by folks on both sides, somewhat aligned with what some researchers have observed regarding cognitive cultural differences (Barbara Götsch, 2014). Each character possesses nuance and depth, offering a unique perspective that enriches the overall story.

The interwoven nature of these characters' stories captures the complexity of personal histories, revealing shared struggles, but it also illuminates broader societal implications tied to the historical context. Shafak seems to employ a delicate balance in her portrayal, showing inner struggles along with external conflicts faced by characters from, generally speaking, diverse backgrounds. She demonstrates how cultural perceptions shape individual experiences, for the most part, effectively. Their interactions and relationships serve as a poignant reflection on a shared history, though one marred by conflict and displacement. This echoes studies on social identity and memory that tend to highlight the emotional connections people form with their cultural past (N Song et al., 2020). By giving voice to characters from different sides of the Turkish-Armenian divide, Shafak invites us to empathise with universally human experiences: longing for connection, grappling with heritage, and the quest for reconciliation amid historical scars.

Themes of Memory and Forgetting

The twin themes of memory and forgetting occupy a key space in Elif Shafak's *The Bastard of Istanbul*, mirroring the tangled threads of history, identity, and individual stories. Shafak skilfully manages the complexities surrounding memory, braiding together personal recollections with communal remembrance, an idea bolstered by scholarship (Martino MLD, 2024) that stresses storytelling's part in moulding shared identities. The novel also explores inherited memories alongside the selective amnesia often linked to historical traumas. Discussions about trauma literature, as you might expect, often highlight how past suffering is both carried forward and strategically forgotten. Through the characters in the story, Shafak makes clear how past events continue to mould current realities, stressing the long shadow cast by unspoken histories – a notion also found in current work on narrative therapy, specifically its focus on how our past influences current identities.

Forgetting, then, isn't a passive act but rather a mechanism, perhaps deliberate, for dealing with complex legacies; it is suggested that forgetting can be strategic in both personal and communal settings (Hansen, J, 2024). The themes of memory and forgetting also meet with the intergenerational transmission of experience, revealing the ways family stories become intertwined within broader historical narratives. Shafak deftly presents the tension between remembering and forgetting, offering a nuanced picture of how individuals and communities grapple with their shared past, which is quite important to grasping the dynamics of historical consciousness. The novel, too, encourages its readers to think about the ethical implications inherent in both remembering and forgetting, thereby prompting reflection on just how historical narratives are built and also the power dynamics that are part and parcel of shaping collective memory, which, broadly speaking, aligns with ongoing conversations we are having about the responsibilities tied to storytelling within society.

Symbolism and Cultural Reflection

Elif Shafak, in The Bastard of Istanbul, intricately weaves together symbolism and cultural reflections, employing various literary techniques to express more profound meanings and spark thought about historical tales. Symbolic elements serve as a connection between individual and shared experiences, allowing readers to relate to broader cultural contexts and past legacies; this mirrors ongoing literary conversations about cultural identity (Tahir S et al., 2024). Through vivid imagery and metaphorical representations, identity, memory, and heritage's complexities are explored, encouraging readers to delve into the interwoven nature of personal lives and larger societal influences—a relevant phenomenon in postmodern literature and philosophical discussions of identity (Uzun M et al., 2022).

Symbols such as the phoenix, the Armenian term hush, and the portrayal of Istanbul itself as a living entity brimming with historical significance all enrich the profound cultural reflection found in the narrative. What's more, the utilisation of symbolism serves to challenge existing norms, shedding light on marginalised narratives. By imbuing the text with layers of symbolic meaning, Shafak—generally speaking—confronts historical silences and encourages critical discussions on contentious topics; this reflects the modern literary exploration of social justice and historical narrative in contemporary fiction (Tahir S et al., 2024). The multi-faceted nature of symbols allows for the exploration of diverse viewpoints and fosters a deeper comprehension of socio-cultural dynamics, which aligns with modern critiques of literature's reflection of societal shifts (Uzun M et al., 2022). When readers navigate this tapestry of symbols, they are compelled to grapple with cultural heritage's complexities and contend with historical interpretation's intricacies, reaffirming literary symbolism's importance in current cultural discourse (Uzun M et al., 2022).

Critics and Reception: Controversies Unfolded

Elif Shafak's *The Bastard of Istanbul* generated considerable discussion upon release, primarily owing to its challenging take on both cultural nuances and how history gets told

(Sharma J, 2024). The novel's reception is quite varied, showing its significant influence on both audiences and those who review books. Some admire Shafak's bravery in tackling difficult subjects, but others take a closer look, sometimes critically, at how the novel portrays Turkish-Armenian links and, specifically, the genocide (J Dybiec-Gajer, 2021).

At its core, the debate around *The Bastard of Istanbul* arises from its direct engagement with historical issues that are often left unspoken, and its characters dealing with the burden of their shared past. Taking apart the different layers of its reception, it is clear that the novel sparks much discussion, triggering dialogues on remembrance, getting past disagreements, and what role literature should play in looking at unresolved historical events. Reviewers have thoroughly examined the book, pointing out Shafak's skill with symbolism and stories with hidden meanings as useful for questioning the usual narratives.

Moreover, the complex characters and the story's web of connections have grabbed readers' attention while also causing lively arguments in literary circles. It seems Shafak's unreserved look at family secrets, the idea of what makes a culture what it is, and fighting for the truth has caused divided opinions both inside and outside the literary world. Even with the problems and censorship it has faced in some places, *The Bastard of Istanbul* continues to be a key topic, which shows how much it still matters in worldwide literature. It's Shafak's talent for creating understanding and encouraging self-reflection through her storytelling that makes the novel so important and lasting. *The Bastard of Istanbul*, in the midst of public opinion and critique, makes clear the undeniable strength of books to question, teach, and bring different viewpoints together.

Comparative Analysis with Previous Works

Looking at Elif Shafak's *The Bastard of Istanbul* alongside her other books offers a chance to see how her storytelling and the themes she cares about have changed, particularly concerning migration and how cultures blend (Barış Ayd Cın, 2024). Shafak is known for mixing detailed history and culture with very personal stories, something that's common in modern books that show multilingual lives (Hansen J, 2024). Unlike her earlier works like *The Flea Palace* and *The Saint of Incipient Insanities*, *The Bastard of Istanbul* deals more directly with tough social and political issues, like the Armenian Genocide. This shows how migration and remembering the past can change a story (Barış Ayd Cın, 2024). This comparison aims to explain the subtle differences and similarities between these books, shedding light on Shafak's growth as a writer and cultural observer as she handles tricky identities and histories.

When put next to her previous stories, *The Bastard of Istanbul* is notable for bravely addressing historical topics often avoided and showing the complicated effects of trauma passed down through generations, which sparks a conversation about how the past affects who we are today (Hansen J, 2024). Through this comparison, it's clear that Shafak's themes have become deeper, moving from smaller, family-based stories to bigger social discussions, all while keeping the detailed characters and storytelling she's famous for. Furthermore, this analysis will explore how the use of symbols and metaphors has changed in her books, helping us better grasp the cultural forces in her stories and further prove her skill as a writer (Barış Ayd Cın, 2024).

Contributions to Contemporary Discourse

Generally speaking, Elif Shafak's novel, *The Bastard of Istanbul*, makes a noteworthy contribution to current conversations concerning historical silences, cultural memory, and, of course, identity. Shafak, through her narrative skills and thematic exploration, delves into complex socio-political issues that resonate quite globally, arguably positioning her work to encourage critical conversations and introspection (Shafak, 2006, p. 45). Shafak's portrayal—meticulous as it is—of characters from diverse cultural backgrounds sheds light on the interconnectedness of human experiences, as well as the lasting impact of historical traumas. Indeed, this resonates with themes of displacement and emplacement discussed in contemporary migration studies (Naeem M et al., 2024). By interweaving, quite skilfully, the Turkish-Armenian heritage into her storytelling, she challenges prevalent narratives and pushes boundaries in addressing historical taboos with nuance and compassion (Shafak, 2006, p. 132). This fosters empathy and understanding; it creates, in fact, a platform where multiple perspectives can coexist, relatively harmoniously, within literature. The Bastard of Istanbul also serves as a poignant reflection on memory and forgetting, urging readers to confront the complexities inherent in personal and collective recollection. As observed in studies of cultural memory (Naeem M et al., 2024), Shafak adeptly navigates the interplay between memory, history, and fiction, thereby inviting a reevaluation of rather entrenched beliefs and motivations.

Her ability to intertwine symbolic elements with historical truths not only enriches the storytelling—that's obvious—but elevates the discourse as well, offering a lens through which current societal dilemmas may be examined and contextualised. In literary criticism, Shafak's work has sparked thought-provoking dialogue, scholars and intellectuals engaging with its implications; her narrative technique contributes to ongoing discussions about the ethical responsibility of literature in confronting historical injustices, and also shaping cultural reckonings (Carole A Martin et al., 2024).

As such, *The Bastard of Istanbul* has become an indispensable reference point for scholars and students seeking to comprehend the multifaceted dimensions of cultural representation, including the power dynamics embedded therein. Moreover, Shafak's contributions extend beyond her narratives. Her advocacy for social justice, human rights, and intercultural dialogue reinforces the relevance of *The Bastard of Istanbul* within broader discussions on inclusivity and equity, as seen in her critical engagement with Sufi philosophy (Naeem M et al., 2024). Through her literary endeavours, Shafak catalyses a greater understanding of cultural hybridity/intersectionality, cultivating an environment where diverse voices converge to illuminate and celebrate the intricacies of human existence. So, ultimately, Elif Shafak's *The Bastard of Istanbul* stands as a beacon of intellectual vigour and artistic prowess, elucidating complex themes and contributing significantly to contemporary discourses on historical silence, memory, and cross-cultural understanding, situating her work, accordingly, within a conversation about legacies of past traumas, including the narratives we construct around them (Carole A Martin et al., 2024).

7
Magical Realism and Beyond
Defining a Genre

Magical Realism and Beyond: Defining a Genre

Magical realism, a transformative genre in literature, transcends simple fantasy. It ingeniously merges the extraordinary and the everyday, allowing the impossible to coexist with what we perceive as real. This unique genre, notably represented by authors like Elif Shafak, serves as a powerful tool for exploring the intricate nature of cultural identity and the experience of living between different worlds. Shafak's stories often illuminate these transitional spaces common in post-colonial settings. In these contexts, magical elements are interwoven with traditional realism, pushing the boundaries of perception and belief. This fusion isn't just for narrative enhancement; it also offers a profound commentary on societal issues and the essence of humanity. The interplay between these dimensions, as seen in both the systematic and paratextual aspects of her work, is a testament to the genre's transformative power. For example, we see it in how her characters are portrayed and the underlying themes in her stories, which resonate with the duality of belonging and alienation (Simge Yılmaz, 2023). So, magical realism isn't just a writing style; it's a potent means to facilitate cultural translation. It allows us to delve into these topics in a nuanced way, exploring the complex realities we face in our globalised world (Clark, G., 2023).

Magical realism is a literary genre that dares to challenge the ordinary and the fantastical, blurring the lines between reality and imagination. The term' magical realism' was first coined by a German art critic, Franz Roh, in 1925. However, it truly blossomed as an artistic movement in Latin American literature. It then transcended those boundaries to influence literature globally. This genre, with its audacious weaving of fantastical events into realistic settings, questions our conventional understanding of reality and offers a significant commentary on the socio-political environments that frame these stories (Simge Yılmaz, 2023). Moreover, magical realism encourages readers to embrace the improbable. It also serves as a method for exploring complex subjects such as identity, cultural background, and the intersection of time and memory. It truly engages readers with the text, prompting them to reconsider the world and the many layers of reality within it (Clark, G., 2023). In essence, this genre challenges us to rethink our concept of reality. In most cases, it pushes the boundaries of what we can perceive and what stories can plausibly tell, all while enriching the literary world with its unique and stimulating presence.

Exploring identity, heritage, and how society works often occurs when the ordinary blends with the bizarre, and this is evident in numerous modern books. When authors delve into unusual topics but keep things relatively normal, it's an opportunity to think deeply and question things, allowing readers to connect with the story in different ways. Authors employ this method to convey profound ideas and spiritual concepts, skilfully blending what's real with what's not, which makes reading more engaging (see Hansen, J., 2024, p. 25). This mix of reality and imagination also allows writers to examine social issues and cultural expectations, providing a means to understand complex situations, as seen in analyses of modern poems and stories (refer to Clark G, 2023, p. 40). Generally speaking, this careful setup doesn't just make books deeper; it also prompts us to reflect on our own lives and the complex story of being human.

Historical Roots: Latin American Influences

To truly grasp magical realism, it is essential to delve into its origins, particularly within Latin American literature. Latin America boasts a rich history steeped in narrative – a blend of indigenous beliefs, colonial experiences, and diverse cultures that form a vibrant storytelling environment (Carole A. Martin et al., 2024). This multicultural mix, generally speaking, fostered magical realism; here, European traditions mingled with indigenous folklore, resulting in a unique style that blurs the line between the real and the fantastic. Think of it this way: the everyday infused with wonder. In the 20th century, authors such as Borges, García Márquez, and Allende championed magical realism, bringing global recognition to this captivating literary form. Their works illuminated Latin American societies, capturing their cultural identity while, in most cases, reaching beyond geographical borders (Thomas Kühne et al., 2023). Through narrative, these literary figures transformed magical realism from a regional style into a global force that continues to impact contemporary literature.

One might argue that the roots of Latin American magical realism lie in the region's complex history – conquest, colonisation, and the clash of civilisations. This collision of worldviews set the stage for narratives that questioned the boundaries between reality and myth. This challenge to conventional truth is a recurring theme. This history, combined with social dynamics, gave magical realism a profound socio-political dimension. It enabled authors to convey allegories and critiques through enchanting stories. Moreover, Latin American magical realism, in general, draws inspiration from the region's social, political, and economic struggles. This presents a unique perspective on the human condition. By weaving the extraordinary into the ordinary, authors used magical realism to explore oppression, resilience, and collective memory. It amplified marginalised voices and shed light on the legacies of colonialism and authoritarian rule. The historical roots of Latin American magical realism lie at its heart in a literary legacy set against a backdrop of cultural diversity, colonial encounters, and socio-political change. This shapes an artistic movement that resonates with readers worldwide, providing pathways for understanding the complex interplay between culture and history.

Elif Shafak's Interpretation of Magical Realism

Elif Shafak deftly incorporates magical realism into her literary works, presenting a distinctive approach shaped by her multicultural background and individual viewpoint. Shafak's magical realism differs somewhat from conventional portrayals; it seamlessly blends mystical and spiritual elements drawn from her Turkish heritage with explorations of contemporary social concerns. The outcome is a compelling blend of the mundane and the fantastical. Her stories spark curiosity while also investigating the intricacies of human nature and society. Shafak's approach stands out through the smooth incorporation of cultural symbols, myths, and folklore into daily life. This technique has been explored in more recent literary criticism (Simge Yılmaz, 2023). Drawing influence from various sources, such as Sūfī poetry, Ottoman history, and Anatolian folklore, she imbues her narratives with a rich array of imagery and symbolism, which often resonates strongly within the framework of both past and present narratives (Clark, G., 2023). The result is a vibrant, multi-layered story that seems to transcend both geographical and temporal boundaries, encouraging readers to consider the interactions between what is tangible and what is not — a feature that aligns closely with broader topics in multicultural literature.

Shafak's take on magical realism, in most cases, serves as a means to address key themes such as identity, displacement, a sense of belonging, and the tension between traditional customs and modern life (Hansen J, 2024). She combines fantastical elements with real-life images of people facing difficult situations. This reveals the complexity of our feelings and struggles, offering a profound insight into what it means to be human. Additionally, Shafak employs magical realism effectively to challenge our conventional perceptions and expand the scope of our stories (Fuller K, 2023). The way she employs this style enables her to paint detailed pictures of relationships and how society functions, doing so in a way that captures your attention and evokes an emotional response. She is quite skilled at using fantastical elements, not only to tell captivating stories but also to evoke emotions and inspire empathy for others, which helps us understand what it means to be human in a more profound way. Generally speaking, Elif Shafak's idea of magical realism goes beyond the usual limits of books. It connects with people everywhere and celebrates the beauty of different cultures. Her skill in blending the ordinary with the unusual demonstrates the power of stories, reaffirming that literature can always bridge gaps and reveal the common experiences we all share.

Themes and Motifs in Her Work

Elif Shafak's literary work is, it's safe to say, quite rich in diverse themes and ideas, reflecting her clear interest in social and political matters, cultural issues, and the full range of human emotions. Her books often explore questions of identity, the feeling of not belonging, and displacement, which she examines closely in stories set in modern times that resonate with her audience. Through the lives of her characters, she examines how individual and group identities intersect, often drawing inspiration from her own multicultural background, as recent discussions about translingual writing have highlighted (Hansen, J, 2024). Stories about being exiled, the diaspora, and the search for a home are important in her books, striking a chord with readers who are also grappling with questions of place and belonging. Besides focusing on personal stories, Shafak also cleverly incorporates larger social issues, such as gender inequality, social injustice, and historical trauma, which align with critical analyses of modern literary expressions (Simge Yılmaz, 2023). Her careful depiction of these themes provides insightful commentary on society. It encourages readers to understand the difficulties faced by marginalised groups.

Furthermore, themes of mysticism, spirituality, and the power of storytelling run through her works, lending them a dreamlike quality that transcends the everyday. Shafak's books often feature detailed descriptions of landscapes and cities, which serve as both settings and symbolic backdrops that reflect the emotional states of her characters. These vivid descriptions, full of sensory details, create immersive worlds that pull readers into the centre of her stories. As she explores the depths of human experience, Shafak also grapples with the conflicts between tradition and the present day, blending mythical elements with modern situations. This contrast enables her to address timeless themes while also setting her stories in the complex world we inhabit today. This kind of thematic depth and interwoven ideas helps make Shafak's writing so appealing, encouraging readers to think about universal truths within the interwoven structure of her stories.

Juxtaposition of Reality and Fantasy

Elif Shafak's literary style strikingly blends reality and fantasy. This fusion serves as a powerful means of exploring intricate themes, holding the audience's attention. Indeed, the way she positions these elements next to each other – elements which might seem quite different – helps create narratives that go beyond what is typically expected. In a way, this mirrors the detailed dynamics of displacement and emplacement, concepts explored in current migration studies (Carole A Martin et al., 2024). Shafak weaves magical realism into settings and characters drawn from the real world. In doing so, she creates a universe where the everyday coexists with the fantastical. This invites us, as readers, to rethink how we understand reality. This fusion enables her to explore philosophical questions that prompt thought: questions about identity, human nature, and even the structure of our societies. This multifaceted approach provides the reader with multiple ways to engage with the author's writing. As noted in considerations about how narratives can impact both individual and collective identities, a key part of this juxtaposition lies in its transformative influence over the reader's familiarity and perception (Fuller, K, 2023).

Shafak, generally speaking, weaves fantastical elements into ordinary settings, pushing us to rethink our daily lives. This aligns, in most cases, with the idea that modern stories should mirror the intricacies of multilingual societies (Hansen J, 2024, p. 23). It's more than just making her stories immersive; it sparks introspection and self-discovery, highlighting the transformative power of storytelling. Moreover, Shafak sets reality against fantasy, suggesting that truth can reside in the surreal and the fantastic can offer profound insights into what it means to be human (Carole A Martin et al., 2024, p. 45). It somewhat illustrates how such techniques can be a means of exploring social issues and identity. This blend enables Shafak to explore societal issues, historical events, and cultural dynamics in ways that transcend traditional storytelling, thereby enhancing reader engagement with the text. The narrative world that emerges challenges our assumptions and broadens the scope of what literature can achieve through its innovative approach. Through this intricate play, Shafak inspires a sense of wonder, curiosity, and contemplation, encouraging readers to look deeper and uncover layers of meaning. As readers navigate this reality-fantasy juxtaposition in Shafak's work, they're invited to reimagine their world, embracing ambiguity and mystery as key parts of the human journey. This intentional blurring—the author's style—creates a literary space that is both intellectually stimulating and emotionally resonant, positioning

Shafak as a storyteller who deftly navigates the intersection between reality and fantasy, effectively inviting exploration into the complexities of contemporary existence.

Character Development and Symbolism

Elif Shafak's novels, broadly speaking, employ intricate character development and meaningful symbolism to explore culture, history, and the human psyche. Characters aren't just individuals; they represent societal figures while remaining deeply personal, mirroring, in many cases, Sūfī traditions where individuals are symbolic tools for self-discovery (Assadi J, 2023). Symbolism, interwoven throughout the stories, enriches experiences and overarching ideas as characters grapple with societal issues and universal struggles. Indeed, symbolism becomes a way to examine identity, belonging, and change. Shafak endows characters with complex traits that reflect the human condition. This balance between realism and allegory makes her stories resonate. Symbolic motifs and recurring images lend the narrative layers of meaning, enhancing introspection and reflecting the philosophical contemplation found within Sūfī literature and themes of spiritual inquiry (Tahir S et al., 2024). Her skill at weaving cultural contexts with characters' emotional landscapes, showing how journeys evoke societal reflections, is underscored by the interplay of character and symbolism. This fusion enables readers to traverse physical and spiritual realms, prompting something more profound than simple storytelling. Through these devices, Shafak prompts readers to recognise universal experiences and the shared importance of connections, engaging them with thought-provoking literature that resonates and elevates discussions of modern identity.

Narrative Techniques and Literary Style

Elif Shafak's storytelling prowess hinges significantly on her narrative techniques and her distinct literary style, solidifying her position as a leading, forward-thinking voice in modern literature (Hansen J, 2024). She is adept at weaving together different narratives, effortlessly combining various viewpoints and time periods. This creates a rich tapestry of linked stories that truly connect with readers, mirroring the multifaceted nature of contemporary existence (Zahra S et al., 2023). Her skilful command of language, rich imagery, and symbolic elements result in a deeply engaging reading experience that captivates audiences globally. Indeed, Shafak's literary style possesses an evocative and almost poetic nature, often drawing from her multifaceted cultural background. This infuses her writing with a captivating and lyrical quality. Through her meticulous attention to detail and strikingly vivid descriptions, she transports readers to culturally vibrant settings. She brings to life the subtle nuances of human experience in ways that feel intensely personal yet remain universally relatable. Ultimately, this allows her work to engage with broader themes of identity and belonging in our increasingly globalised world.

Elif Shafak, it seems, plays with narrative structure quite a bit. Rather than sticking to a straight line, her stories often weave and wind, much like how memories and feelings actually work (Carole A. Martin et al., 2024). She's into exploring different ways of telling a story, such as circular narratives or presenting things from multiple points of view. This invites us, as readers, to become deeply engaged – both thinking and feeling – and to connect with the characters and their experiences. Contemporary analyses, as you might expect, have picked up on this (Zahra S et al., 2023). This innovative style allows Shafak to go beyond the usual limits of storytelling, offering a rich and thought-provoking experience. She also likes to sprinkle in a bit of magical realism, adding wonder to her tales and blurring the lines between what's real and what's not. This mix of everyday things and the fantastical helps to shed light on bigger truths and questions about life, prompting us to ponder the mysteries of being alive and the resilience of the human spirit. Generally speaking, Shafak's narrative techniques and style showcase her creativity and artistic vision, underscoring her dedication to pushing the limits of modern literature. Ultimately, this encourages readers to embrace all aspects of human existence, building bridges between different cultural stories (Carole A Martin et al., 2024).

Reader Reception and Criticism

The reception and critical analysis of Elif Shafak's works are crucial for understanding their place in literary conversations, particularly considering her use of magical realism.

Learning how readers connect with and interpret Shafak's stories provides us with important insights into the influence of her work and the range of critical opinions it provokes. Shafak's wide-ranging global audience brings a mix of cultural, social, and ideological viewpoints, which is essential for grasping literary inequalities where some languages have more prominence (Julie M. Hansen, 2024). This varied readership leads to diverse interpretations and critiques. A key aspect of reader reception is how Shafak's themes and characters resonate with diverse individuals. Many readers find a connection with her nuanced depictions of cultural identities, social problems, and emotions, leading to personal reflection.

These universal themes enable readers from diverse backgrounds to find common ground, fostering empathy. Engaging with reader criticism provides a valuable insight into how Shafak's work is perceived. Critics and scholars examine the literary qualities, sociopolitical meanings, and philosophical foundations of her texts, fuelling discussions about her storytelling (Hansen J, 2024). Through critical analysis, readers are encouraged to question assumptions and consider the human experience presented by Shafak. Literary criticism also helps readers explore more profound meanings within Shafak's narratives, revealing subtle allegories. This exploration provides a deeper understanding of her writing, thereby enriching the reading experience. Examining reader reception and criticism reveals the dynamic relationship between author, text, and audience, illustrating how literature can influence both individual and collective awareness. Overall, studying reader reception and criticism provides a means to appreciate Elif Shafak's enduring impact. By showing the varied interpretations and critical engagements with her works, it underscores literature's power to bridge divides, foster empathy, and spark dialogue. In conclusion, examining reader reception and criticism reveals the enduring impact of Shafak's narratives on engaging and uniting readers within the global literary community.

Comparative Analysis with Contemporary Authors

Elif Shafak's literary contributions position her as a significant voice in modern literature; her works distinguish themselves through narrative innovation and thematic exploration, aligning with current discussions in literary spheres, particularly concerning multilingual perspectives (Hansen J, 2024). Analysing her work in relation to her contemporaries offers a perspective on her unique role in reflecting and reshaping societal standards. Investigating her collection of works alongside fellow authors unveils recurring themes related to cultural identity and diasporic experiences, mirroring larger critical dialogues regarding language dynamics and ethnic identity. This study is further illuminated by considering the literature's function as a reflector of historical and modern socio-political environments, emphasising the significance of trauma and cultural heritage in novels addressing events such as the Armenian Genocide (Thomas Kühne et al., 2023). Placing Shafak within this wider conversation acknowledges her personal contribution. It highlights the connections that link her thematically with other prominent authors of today.

Examining magical realism in Elif Shafak's works, it's useful to compare her to other contemporary writers who employ this style. Reflecting on how Shafak's work aligns with that of Isabel Allende, Salman Rushdie, and Gabriel García Márquez helps us understand what makes each author unique. For example, Allende often mixes magical realism with political and social issues in Latin America. Rushdie, on the other hand, blends real historical events with fantastical elements, showcasing complex cultural and religious themes – a trend observed where trauma intersects with identity (Ralph J. Poole, 2022). Then there's Gabriel García Márquez, known for making the everyday seem extraordinary in Macondo, his fictional town. His emphasis on the links between myth and reality is also evident in Shafak's stories. Shafak, with her Turkish background and global perspective, combines magical elements with social commentary and thoughtful stories, demonstrating the importance of culture in shaping writing (Finlay F, 2020). This kind of comparison helps us understand Shafak better. Additionally, it highlights the variety and subtle differences in magical realism across the world.

Additionally, when we examine the themes, characters, and writing styles of these authors, we uncover complex, symbolic stories that have transcended borders and resonated with readers worldwide. Moreover, such analysis highlights how magical realism has evolved as a genre, adapting and resonating in various cultures. Through this exploration, we can appreciate the universal themes and human stories hidden in the complex tales of modern authors, revealing our shared human experience in diverse mythologies and imaginative spaces.

Conclusion: Beyond Magical Realism

In wrapping up our exploration of magical realism and its influence on contemporary literature, it becomes clear that Elif Shafak's work transcends a single genre. People have linked her writing to magical realism, sure. However, really, Shafak's way of telling stories goes past simple labels, showing us a much bigger picture that doesn't fit neatly into any box (Shafak, 2006, p. 45). Her stories blend what's real with what's not, offering profound insights into what it means to be human, how society functions, and the complex aspects of our cultural backgrounds (Alshehri et al., 2022). She skilfully weaves together magical elements with everyday life, prompting us to consider profound truths and explore a wide range of human experiences in ways that resonate with people from diverse cultures.

Additionally, Shafak can seamlessly blend magical elements with social and political commentary and historical references, demonstrating the numerous layers her books possess (Furlanetto et al., 2017). Her way of structuring stories isn't just about fun, imaginary worlds; it's also a strong way to question power, fight against old unfairness, and stand up for those who don't usually get heard. So, her storytelling extends beyond just the cool, attractive aspects of magical realism; it helps us examine ourselves and address issues collectively. Additionally, by exploring themes such as identity, feeling lost, and discovering one's place, Shafak's books transcend the boundaries of a genre, touching us deeply with human emotions and questions about our purpose. Through her well-developed characters and stories rich in symbolism, she delves into what we think about as individuals and as a society, making a lasting impact that extends far beyond simply being labelled as magical realism. Because she explores a wide range of topics, Shafak's work prompts us to reconsider what genres even mean, encouraging us to be more open and view books in a broader context. It asks us to love all the cool and different aspects of storytelling, understanding that the lines between genres aren't hard and fast, allowing stories to evolve and grow. Generally speaking, as we look past the limits of magical realism, we find ourselves in a world of books that celebrate our big imaginations, question society, and speak poignantly about what it means to be human.

8
Rumi and Shams
Exploring Love and Mysticism in Fiction

Introduction to Rumi and Shams: Historical Context and Literary Influence

Jalal ad-Din Muhammad Rumi, often simply known as Rumi, the 13th-century Persian poet, jurist, and theologian, had a profound impact on literature, spirituality, and philosophy that still resonates today (Naeem M et al., 2024). Born in what is now Afghanistan, he later lived in Konya, Turkey. Rumi's poems truly capture the essence of Sufi mysticism, love, and the spiritual quest. His famous Masnavi remains a central work in Persian literature, offering insights into what it means to be human and the search for divine unity (Tariq S et al., 2023). Just as important is Shams-i-Tabrizi, a dervish who travelled around and became Rumi's mentor, significantly changing Rumi's life. Their unusual connection highlights the concept of two souls being deeply intertwined and has sparked numerous artistic and literary interpretations. Shams' disappearance, which was quite mysterious, and the subsequent quest to find him again spiritually, have made their story even more captivating. Historically speaking, the relationship between Rumi and Shams transcends the typical teacher-student dynamic.

In most cases, it reveals a profound interplay between the mind, emotions, and a strong spiritual desire. Moreover, Rumi and Shams have had an influence that extends far beyond Persian and Turkish culture. Their lasting impact has spread throughout the world, generally encouraging a love for Sufi poetry, contemplation of love, and the pursuit of enlightenment within oneself. Even now, their work continues to inspire writers, academics, and those seeking spiritual growth, offering them a way to contemplate universal love, divine knowledge, and spiritual truths. The convergence of classical wisdom and modern interpretations highlights the enduring importance of Rumi and Shams, solidifying their place as figures whose cultural significance transcends time and place (Naeem M et al., 2024). All things considered, the intertwined stories of Rumi and Shams emphasise that love is a transformative power, reminding us of the deep human need to connect and understand, both spiritually and in our daily lives (Tariq S et al., 2023).

The Mystical Bond: Understanding the Relationship Between Rumi and Shams

The enduring mystique surrounding the relationship between Rumi, the celebrated Persian poet, and Shams Tabriz, his spiritual guide, still fascinates readers and academics. Their connection, at its core, embodies a profound spiritual affinity that exceeds typical understandings of human bonds, a dynamic that Shafak examines through the lens of love and spirituality (Naeem et al., 2024). Understanding this mystical partnership necessitates examining the historical and philosophical backdrop of their friendship. Rumi, the esteemed Sufi mystic and poet, discovered in Shams a compatible soul, whose unconventional teachings sparked a transformative voyage of self-discovery.

The wandering dervish, Shams, presented Rumi with a

novel viewpoint, challenging his established convictions and prompting an exploration into divine love and spiritual insight, further detailed in Shafak's initial six principles of spiritual love (Tariq S et al., 2023). Their interaction embodies more than just an intellectual exchange; it marks a merging of souls on a higher plane, where individual identities dissolve in the pursuit of ultimate truth. Often, this profound connection is portrayed as a symbolic portrayal of the seeker and the guide, an illustration of the age-old pursuit for enlightenment and union with the divine. We gain insight into the intricacies of their relationship, as well as its profound influence on Rumi's poetic articulation and spiritual development, by examining their dialogues and correspondence. This intense intellectual and emotional exchange showcases the magnetic pull between master and disciple, a poignant reminder of the transformative capability inherent in profound spiritual connections as well as the path to enlightenment, shedding light on the many facets of their legendary partnership.

Symbolism of Love in Rumi's Poetry: A Literary Analysis

Jalal ad-Din Muhammad Rumi, the Persian poet and mystic of the 13th century, frequently returned to the theme of love in his work. His poetry, you see, deeply explores the complexities of what it means to be human and to feel, with love really being at the heart of it all. Love, as Rumi presents it, isn't just about romance or physical attraction; it's more like a universal power, something that goes beyond the limits of our world and connects to the divine love that you find discussed in Sufi literature (Tahir S et al., 2024). Through his intricate use of metaphors and allegories, Rumi effectively conveys the spiritual significance of love, portraying it as a transformative force that unites and brings things together. The images and symbols he uses serve as profound metaphysical expressions, inviting us, the readers, to embark on our own journey of introspection and self-discovery. Rumi's concept of love as a divine force, one that connects us to something greater than ourselves, remains resonant with people across diverse cultures and generations. It also aligns with modern discussions about the subject (Assadi J, 2023).

The symbolism of love in Rumi's poetry extends far beyond simple affection. It shows love as something that awakens you from within and helps you grow spiritually. Suppose you examine the various symbols and motifs Rumi employs. In that case, you can find layers of meaning that help you better understand what it means to be human and to search for something beyond the everyday. Throughout his work, Rumi employs symbols such as the beloved, wine, and the tavern, each with its own complex meaning. The beloved, often used as a stand-in for the divine, is like an eternal source of spiritual affection and guidance, drawing people toward self-discovery and unity with the divine. Similarly, the images of wine and the tavern represent the intoxicating nature of divine love and the spiritual high one feels when trying to connect with the divine. When you look closely at these symbols, you begin to see Rumi's intricate portrayal of love as a transformative force, one that elevates human consciousness and breaks down the barriers between the material and the metaphysical.

Furthermore, Rumi's symbolism of love also includes ideas about unity, harmony, and letting go of the ego, emphasising how everything is connected, which highlights the Sufi tradition's emphasis on unity (Tahir S et al., 2024). His poetic vision encourages us to consider the limitless nature of love and its profound impact on our souls. Through a literary analysis of the symbolism of love in Rumi's poetry, one can discern the timeless relevance of his insights, offering profound wisdom that transcends cultural and temporal boundaries, affirming the continued exploration of these themes in modern literature (Assadi J, 2023).

Elif Shafak's Interpretation of Rumi's Legacy in Modern Fiction

Elif Shafak's books delve into Rumi's lasting impact, exploring love, mysticism, and spiritual growth in depth, as many critics have noted (Friedman SS, 2018). Shafak subtly incorporates Rumi's ideas into her stories, carefully showing characters as they find themselves. It's almost as if she aims to spark a conversation between then and now. Shafak reimagines Rumi's profound wisdom for today, inviting us on a personal journey that transcends time and place, forging a connection to mystical traditions. Shafak cleverly blends historical mysticism with modern thinking, linking the past to the present – a key theme she explores (Cheang S., et al., 2020).

Indeed, her rendering of Rumi's wisdom strikes a chord,

evoking a sense of shared humanity. In a way, Shafak both honours Rumi and makes his wisdom new for today, casting herself as a modern keeper of old wisdom. Shafak's knack for weaving Rumi's teachings into her modern fiction demonstrates just how timeless his insights are, perhaps challenging our notions about literary genres and spiritual discourse. Through transformative experiences, Shafak expresses the call for love and introspection that mysticism embodies, situating her work as vital to the ongoing discourse surrounding spirituality in literature.

Mysticism as a Narrative Device: Bridging Past and Present

Elif Shafak often employs mysticism as a compelling narrative tool, particularly when examining the intertwined lives of Rumi and Shams. Drawing from Sufism's mystical traditions—encompassing divine love, spiritual union, and the pursuit of enlightenment—Shafak cleverly bridges the past and present. This creates a rich storytelling tapestry that really resonates with contemporary readers. In, say, *The Forty Rules of Love*, Shafak expertly navigates the complexities of mysticism, weaving together historical accounts and mythical elements. She blurs the lines, seemingly seamlessly, between reality and those more metaphysical experiences. Through Shams, a rather enigmatic character, she brings the essence of the Sufi tradition to light, not just as a historical figure, but also as a symbol of spiritual mentorship and transformative love.

Furthermore, Shafak's depiction of mysticism in her narratives extends beyond religious or philosophical connotations. Instead, it becomes a powerful instrument for addressing those universal themes of human existence—such as the search for truth, the nature of relationships, and the intrinsic search for meaning. The mystical journey her characters undertake reflects a profound introspection into the human condition, offering readers a lens through which to contemplate their own personal and spiritual quests. Moreover, by employing mysticism as a narrative device, Shafak juxtaposes the timeless wisdom of Rumi and Shams with contemporary societal dilemmas, thereby highlighting the relevance of their teachings to the modern world. Through allegorical storytelling and those rather profound philosophical insights, she prompts readers to reevaluate their perceptions of love, spirituality, and interconnectedness. This makes mystical traditions accessible and applicable in today's globalised society. Shafak's skilful integration of mysticism in her narratives doesn't just act as a bridge between past and present. However, it also fosters a more profound understanding of cultural heritage and spiritual wisdom, in most cases. By intertwining these elements, she creates a compelling dialogue that transcends temporal boundaries, inviting readers to embark on a transformative journey, in a sense, of self-discovery and empathy. Ultimately, mysticism becomes more than just a thematic backdrop, emerging as a catalyst for profound reflection. It encourages a harmonious convergence of both ancient wisdom and contemporary consciousness.

Characterisation of Shams: Perspectives Through Shafak's Lens

Shams of Tabriz, that rather mysterious individual who had such a profound impact on Rumi, has captured imaginations for a long time. We will explore how Elif Shafak presents Shams, specifically within the framework of Sufism and identity (Nahid S et al., 2025). Shafak's rendering offers various layers, going beyond a straightforward account to reveal a person of contradictions and, indeed, profound understanding. Through skilful writing and character building, Shafak unveils the multifaceted nature of Shams, illuminating his spiritual insight, as well as his unusual actions, and the profound shift he caused in Rumi's life, further explained in her study of gender dynamics and societal pressures (Zahra AFA'a, 2020). Shams becomes this agent of change in Rumi's spiritual growth, representing a combination of love and wisdom that questions established traditions. This detailed portrayal encourages readers to consider the wider philosophical and cultural meanings of Shams, and it really emphasises why Shafak's story matters in understanding the complexities of human relationships and spiritual enlightenment.

Exploring Themes of Spiritual Transformation and Quest for Knowledge

For those engaged in introspection and seeking personal growth, Shams serves almost as a symbol, representing both spiritual awakening and, perhaps, unorthodox wisdom. Shafak, through her descriptions and dialogues, elucidates the evolution of Shams's relationship with Rumi, and in doing so, interweaves mystical elements with very human vulnerabilities. She presents Shams not as a flawless sage, but as a flawed, yet still compelling figure; his teachings seeming to emanate from a place of deep authenticity. As some scholars have noted while analysing Shafak's work, her portrayal of Shams often resonates on multiple levels, subtly encouraging a dialogue about the complexities inherent in spiritual teachings within a modern context (Naeem M et al., 2024). Through Shafak's lens, Shams becomes like a mirror, one reflecting the inner conflicts and aspirations of the characters—and indeed the readers. The portrayal, generally speaking, goes beyond mere historical depictions, inviting readers to contemplate the universal themes of love, devotion, and the existential pursuit of meaning.

Shafak's characterisation of Shams offers a fresh interpretation, one that transcends cultural boundaries and thus resonates with audiences irrespective of their familiarity with Sufi literature. This in-depth examination of Shafak's portrayal of Shams reveals the intricate layers of both mysticism and human connection within her narrative, enriching the discourse on spirituality and personal transformation within the broader context of her literary oeuvre. Within the realm of Elif Shafak's literary landscape, the exploration of spiritual transformation—and that insatiable quest for knowledge—emerges as a pervasive theme that, in most cases, transcends both cultural boundaries and temporal constraints. Shafak masterfully navigates these themes, delving into the depths of human consciousness and the interconnectedness of spiritual experiences across her diverse narratives. The transformative power of spirituality is intricately woven into the very fabric of her storytelling, guiding readers through an introspective journey that seems to transcend the limitations of conventional thought. Central to this exploration of spiritual transformation is, of course, the notion of inner awakening and enlightenment. Shafak skilfully crafts characters who undergo profound metamorphoses, embarking on quests that lead them to confront their deepest fears, desires, and even their existential quandaries. Through these transformative journeys, she illuminates the universal yearning for self-discovery and the pursuit of higher truths, echoing themes found in both classic works of Sufi literature and also contemporary interpretations that invite reflection (Tahir S., et al., 2024).

Moreover, Shafak intertwines the theme of spiritual transformation with the relentless pursuit of knowledge, undertaking a nuanced examination of the intersection between faith, philosophy, and intellectual enlightenment. Her works serve as conduits through which the complexities of mystical experiences and the intellectual pursuit of truth converge, in turn fostering an enriching dialogue on the symbiotic relationship between spirituality and cognition. In essence, Shafak's portrayal of spiritual transformation, as well as the quest for knowledge, extends beyond narrative devices, serving instead as a contemplative reflection of the human condition. Through her prose, she invites readers to explore the intricate tapestries of existence, inviting introspection and fostering a deeper understanding of the forces that shape our perceptions of reality. By seamlessly interweaving the ethereal with the tangible, Shafak imparts a profound sense of interconnectedness, igniting a collective exploration of the perennial themes that seem to permeate the human experience. As readers traverse the landscapes of Shafak's literary oeuvre, they are encouraged to embark on their own journeys of self-discovery and intellectual expansion. The indelible impression left by these themes of spiritual transformation and the pursuit of knowledge underscores Shafak's prowess as a storyteller, one who not only entertains but also elevates the consciousness of her audience by instilling a lasting reverence for the boundless dimensions of human existence.

The Intersection of Philosophy and Fiction: Unravelling Mystical Concepts

Elif Shafak, in her exploration of the mystical ideas found in the works of Rumi and Shams, artfully combines philosophy and fiction. This blending serves to uncover deep mystical layers, a feat achieved by drawing from the wellspring of Sufism. This tradition has notably shaped the perspectives of numerous authors throughout time (Naeem et al., 2024). A subtle equilibrium typically exists at this intersection; it's a balance between rational thinking and spiritual quest. Indeed, Shafak constructs narratives that challenge conventional views on existence and transcendence, reflecting the complex interplay between intellect and divine love —a common theme in Sufi doctrine (Tahir S., et al., 2024). Her narratives, particularly her evocative storytelling, delve into the territory of the genuine and the shared human experience, emphasising love's capacity to transform and awaken spirits. Shafak, by embedding elements of Sufism within the lives of her characters, encourages us, the readers, to rethink the limitations of faith, logic, and our own personal development, resonating, in a way, with the enduring sagacity of Rumi's philosophical investigations, all while giving a current viewpoint from which we can grasp spiritual quandaries (Naeem M., et al., 2024).

Elif Shafak's work, in many ways, showcases the complex interplay between love and mysticism, drawing on Sufi philosophy to highlight the interconnectedness of all beings, both in our everyday lives and in the more spiritual realms. She gives her characters philosophical depth, which allows readers to engage with profound questions about what it means to be and to be aware - ideas often explored in studies focusing on Sufi themes in literature (Naeem M., et al., 2024). In Shafak's stories, this back-and-forth between philosophy and fiction becomes a way to delve into some of life's great mysteries. She weaves mystical ideas into her writing, thoughtfully examining metaphysical themes and genuinely embracing the complex interplay of human emotions, alongside our universal quest for meaning (Tahir S., et al., 2024).

Shafak's knack for incorporating philosophical thoughts doesn't just make her stories richer; it pulls readers into a thoughtful exploration, making them question what they already believe and inviting some self-reflection. And, by bringing philosophy and fiction together, she's able to shed light on the really transcendent aspects of mystical experiences. Through her prose, generally speaking, she captures the essence of metaphysical ideas, depicting the transformative effect of spiritual awakening and how it resonates across time and space. Through detailed symbolism and motifs, she creates a story that transcends conventional storytelling, delving deep into our innermost thoughts and evoking the timeless appeal of transcendental wisdom.

Shafak's skilful navigation of these philosophical ideas within her stories widens the horizons of literature and creates a fitting space for considering some profound existential questions. Her work, this thought-provoking combination of mystical concepts and philosophical musings, invites readers to participate in a conversation that extends beyond mere reading, sparking a kind of intellectual exchange that truly resonates with what it means to be human. Philosophy, then, isn't just a theory; it becomes part of the story itself, weaving together a tapestry of mystical narratives that, in most cases, echo with deep insights and wisdom. This, arguably, establishes Shafak's work as an important exploration of Sufi thought and its underlying themes.

Cultural Impact: How 'The Forty Rules of Love' Redefined Romantic Narratives

Elif Shafak's "The Forty Rules of Love" has made a lasting impression, almost sparking a cultural revival in how we think about romantic stories. By cleverly weaving together the mystical wisdom of Rumi and the life-changing power of love, Shafak actually goes beyond typical storytelling, redefining what romance means today (Naeem M., et al., 2024). The way she portrays different characters undergoing spiritual awakenings and deep desires draws readers into a world where love isn't limited by societal expectations or the passage of time. One key impact of "The Forty Rules of Love" is that it challenges traditional notions of romance. Shafak avoids the usual clichés, instead capturing a deeper sense of love. She challenges us to see love as a spiritual and intellectual bond, not just a passing feeling (Fuller K, 2023). This fresh take on romance has captured readers' attention and sparked conversations about how genuine, soulful connections can transform modern relationships. Plus, the book's complex characters and storytelling have opened up new ground in showing love across different cultures.

Shafak artfully blends the stories of Ella Rubinstein and Aziz Zahara, creating a poignant blend of Western and Eastern perspectives on love and spirituality. This thoughtful approach fosters cross-cultural understanding and highlights the shared human experience, as well as the search for something greater through love. Readers worldwide have connected with its exploration of cultural meeting points, prompting reflection on the common threads that unite us. In addition, "The Forty Rules of Love" has helped bring Sufi philosophy and literature back into the spotlight, reintroducing Rumi's timeless wisdom to a modern audience. Shafak's skilful storytelling walks readers through profound philosophical and spiritual ideas, sparking a new appreciation for Rumi's teachings (Naeem M., et al., 2024). It acts as a catalyst, generally speaking, for those seeking a more enlightened perspective.

Conclusion: The Enduring Legacy of Mysticism in Contemporary Storytelling

Contemporary storytelling's engagement with mysticism reveals a lasting impact on both literature and our understanding of ourselves. Elif Shafak's narratives, especially, offer a glimpse into how mystical traditions continue to shape our modern perspectives (Kuyucu N, 2020). "The Forty Rules of Love" stands as proof of mysticism's powerful ability to redefine romance and deepen our insight into human relationships. Shafak's portrayal of Rumi, the Sufi poet, and Shams, his guide, breathes new life into the age-old master-disciple dynamic, drawing readers into a contemplative experience filled with love and wisdom (Friedman SS, 2018). This narrative strength extends beyond conventional stories, enriching contemporary literature with a shared language of the heart.

Mysticism, as Shafak represents it, bridges cultures and eras, mirroring the ongoing quest for inner peace. Her fiction highlights the search for spiritual truth as a vital element of the human experience, intertwined with the complexities of life. The inclusion of mystical elements, generally speaking, into today's literature amplifies the connection between what we can touch and what we cannot, providing a space where the unspeakable finds expression. This underscores the transformative capacity of mysticism to shed light on the human condition, fostering empathy. As we navigate Shafak's stories, the allure of mystical themes becomes apparent, offering a sense of solace. Indeed, the meeting of ancient wisdom with modern storytelling captivates, igniting a collective desire for transcendence and nurturing a deeper sense of our shared humanity. Thus, the legacy of mysticism serves as a guide, leading us through the soul's labyrinth and inviting us to join the dance of love and spiritual discovery. In conclusion, Shafak's skilful interpretation of mysticism accentuates its importance, ensuring its wisdom continues to enrich the literary landscape for years to come.

9
Narratives of Marginalisation
Giving Voice to the Voiceless

Introduction to Marginalisation in Literature

The narratives concerning marginalisation play a vital role; they amplify the voices of those often unheard, especially when cultural translation comes into play—a field where identity and belonging are, as it were, profoundly intertwined. The works of Elif Shafak are a great example of this examination. Shafak presents complex characters whose experiences reveal the fragmentation and dislocation frequently found in today's world. Through her stories, Shafak generally cultivates an understanding of how people navigate their identities during socio-cultural changes, building dialogue and fostering connections. Her literary contribution reflects the scholarly discussion on emplacement and migration, highlighting the significance of stories that reveal the often-hidden struggles faced by marginalised communities (Carole A. Martin et al., 2024). In addition, this portrayal challenges the monolithic narratives that often dominate mainstream discussions. Instead, she offers a tapestry, you might say, of lived experiences that resonate both collectively and personally. By addressing the intricacies of alienation and belonging, Shafak not only voices those who have been silenced but also encourages the reader to confront the socio-political structures that, in most cases, sustain these dynamics (Fuller K, 2023).

Literature offers a poignant and multifaceted exploration of marginalisation, shedding light on historically unheard voices. It captures the subtleties of their stories, particularly concerning migration and cultural displacement. Think of it as a deep dive into the societal fabric, where narratives of often-overlooked people and communities are carefully woven together. Cultural migration, in a sense, amplifies this understanding; going beyond mere geographical shifts, it shows how marginalised voices enrich the human experience (Barış Ayd Cın, 2024). What's truly central here is recognising the diverse experiences, identities, and struggles often obscured by dominant cultural views, in most cases challenging what we consider conventional stories and thus offering novel routes for understanding (Martino MLD, 2024). Through this intricate acknowledgement, literature turns into a potent instrument of social reflection, empowering marginalised groups to vocalise their lives and stake their claim within the literary world.

Historical Context: Understanding the Roots of Silence

To understand narratives of marginalisation, it's important to consider the historical context and how silence has been woven into society for a long time. Silencing marginalised voices isn't new; it's been happening for centuries, often because of power imbalances, discrimination, and hierarchies. This section aims to shed light on the origins of these silenced narratives, tracing them through history, as noted by. From the suppression of opposition in autocratic systems to the erasure of native viewpoints in colonial times, history provides a broad picture of how dominant narratives interact with marginalised experiences. By understanding these layers, we can start to grasp the long-lasting effects of history on how literature portrays people.

In most cases, understanding the history also helps us examine closely the factors that perpetuate marginalisation, such as prejudices, cultural dominance, and the undervaluing of certain people's lives. A sentiment echoed in the discussions presently looking at these things, we can face the widespread patterns that push marginalised voices to the edge. Also, by recognising these patterns, we can try to undo the historical baggage that keeps silencing these communities. Generally speaking, by looking at the historical roots of silence, we can begin to disrupt established power structures and give centre stage to narratives that have often been ignored. Furthermore, being aware of history empowers both writers and readers to question and challenge current standards, thereby contributing to the creation of a more inclusive literary world. Ultimately, this section delves into the complex history of silencing, revealing the numerous factors that shape how marginalised voices are represented in literature, and reinforcing the need to amplify their stories to create a fairer and more understanding literary environment.

Character Development: Crafting Authentic Voices

Representing marginalised characters authentically in literature demands, as scholars often note, a profound understanding of their lived realities, internal world, and cultural background; doing so helps to capture the nuances inherent in their stories (Hansen, J., 2024, p. 45). More than just narrating an event, it's about exploring the layers of human feeling, the impact of societal forces, and the weight of history, all of which shape who they are. Literary theorists have noted that, through careful attention to character development, authors can shed light on the hardships, strengths, and hopes of those whose voices are often absent from mainstream stories (Clark, G., 2023, p. 78).

When developing these characters, writers should generally approach them with both empathy and sensitivity, recognising the many dimensions to their existence; indeed, this consideration often arises in conversations about ethical representation. This often means conducting extensive research, conducting interviews, and immersing oneself in the communities being represented, all of which help lay a strong foundation for genuine and well-developed characters (Hansen J, 2024, p. 90). By truly capturing the subtle details of how they speak, carry themselves, and think, authors are able to breathe life into their characters; doing so allows readers to connect with them on a profound, human level. Moreover, creating authentic voices also requires understanding how different forms of marginalisation intersect, which reinforces the need to fully comprehend the diverse experiences encountered by these individuals (Clark, G., 2023, p. 112).

Authors must grapple with intertwined challenges stemming from aspects like race, gender, sexual orientation, socioeconomic status, and disability. A nuanced exploration of how these elements intersect and shape a character's lived experience is essential for effective portrayal. By illustrating the complexities inherent in identity, authors can challenge stereotypes and dismantle preconceived notions, thereby contributing to a more inclusive literary landscape. Furthermore, crafting genuine voices requires dedication to depicting the full range of emotions and agency present within marginalised communities. While their reality includes oppression and hardship, it also encompasses moments of joy, love, and even triumph. Authors can affirm the humanity of these characters by showcasing the multifaceted nature of their experiences, thereby empowering readers to empathise with their individual journeys.

The development of characters also involves weaving the cultural richness and traditions of marginalised communities into the fabric of the narrative. These elements – language, rituals, folklore, or familial dynamics – add depth and authenticity to the story. Such inclusion offers readers a glimpse into potentially unfamiliar worlds, promoting cross-cultural understanding and appreciation. Ultimately, the creation of authentic voices for marginalised characters is both a creative pursuit and a moral obligation. This empowers authors not just to tell captivating narratives but also to amplify the voices that have, for too long, remained on the fringes of literature. Through this undertaking, literature has the potential to catalyse empathy, social awareness, and advocacy, ultimately forging a more inclusive and equitable literary canon.

The Role of the Narrator in Highlighting Invisibility

Narrators in literature function as essential conduits, illuminating the experiences of individuals often relegated to the margins. A narrator, through masterful employment of perspective and voice, can expose realities kept hidden from view by prevailing societal norms; this mirrors investigations into women's literary efforts, which aim to construct decentralised knowledge systems that challenge dominant narratives (Martino MLD, 2024). The subsequent discussion explores the complexities inherent in narrative voice and its capacity to give voice to stories that might otherwise remain unheard. Empathy stands as a central concept, where a skilfully drawn narrator has the potential to embody the emotions, struggles, and triumphs of diverse characters.

By probing these characters' inner lives, the narrator becomes an advocate, promoting their visibility and beckoning readers to confront the difficulties they encounter. This sympathetic representation allows readers to develop a more nuanced understanding of the multifaceted aspects of human existence, one that transcends race, gender, and class boundaries. Moreover, the narrator's role in emphasising invisibility involves careful decisions about storytelling methods and literary devices. Whether through utilising stream-of-consciousness narration to convey the inner struggles of a protagonist from a marginalised background, or via multi-perspective narratives that capture the diverse voices within a community, the narrator's art shapes the story's framework, thereby amplifying narratives pushed to the periphery, a phenomenon observed in studies of multilingual storytelling's impact on reader involvement (Hansen J, 2024).

Furthermore, narrators must challenge established prejudices and dismantle stereotypes that perpetuate the marginalisation of particular groups. Through nuanced narrative techniques, the narrator disrupts the prevailing discourse, elucidating the complexities surrounding identity and the intersectional nature of oppression. By doing so, the narrator acts to dismantle barriers, ones that confine marginalised individuals to the periphery of societal recognition, presenting their lives with genuine depth, dignity, and authenticity. Highlighting invisibility via the narrator's role is not only about mere representation but also functions as a call to action. This encourages readers to acknowledge the shared humanity of those relegated to the fringes of social awareness, and it also encourages engagement with stories that question the status quo. By wielding narrative voice, the narrator becomes an instrument for social transformation, prompting readers to confront what remains unseen and amplify the voices that have long been silenced.

Explorations of Gender and Identity

Marginalised narratives in literature are deeply intertwined with explorations of gender and identity. Elif Shafak, generally speaking, demonstrates a deep understanding of these themes, particularly the complexities surrounding gender roles, societal expectations, and the inherent struggle for identity when marginalisation is present (Martino MLD, 2024). Shafak navigates the nuances and challenges faced by marginalised individuals through her characters, whose voices are often silenced – she delves into the multifaceted aspects of gender and identity. Her portrayal transcends binary constraints, as she navigates a spectrum of experiences beyond conventional boundaries.

The characters grapple with societal constructs, ingrained prejudices, and the quest for self-discovery, often facing systemic barriers. Their journeys reflect the intersection of gender and identity with race, class, and culture (Carole A Martin et al., 2024). Shafak illuminates the intricacies of personal identity formation, revealing internal conflicts and external pressures. She also delves into the intersectionality of identity, acknowledging the layers of oppression that compound challenges for marginalised groups. By portraying struggles and triumphs authentically, Shafak prompts readers to confront injustices perpetuated by societal norms. Moreover, her exploration delves into resilience and agency, emphasising self-definition and the impact of community support. Instead of simplistic portrayals, Shafak opts for a textured examination of human experiences. Each character illustrates how gender and identity intersect, interweaving with struggles for empowerment and social justice. Ultimately, Shafak's exploration presents a nuanced portrayal, prompting readers to challenge prevailing notions and advocate for inclusivity and equity. By shedding light on intimate facets of gender and identity, Shafak's work inspires empathy, understanding, and a commitment to amplifying silenced voices.

Socioeconomic Disparities: Bridging the Class Divide

Generally speaking, socioeconomic disparities essentially set the stage in literature, influencing the stories and lives of the characters we meet. Examining this class divide presents a unique opportunity for authors; they can illuminate the complex nature of social stratification and its impact on both individuals and entire communities. Through nuanced storytelling techniques, authors navigate the complexities of privilege and deprivation, highlighting the often unseen barriers that impact access to resources, opportunities, and power. Crafting characters from diverse socioeconomic backgrounds enables writers to explore the connections between class, race, gender, and other key identity markers, which are essential for understanding the multifaceted contemporary realities (Guerry et al., 2013). By portraying the actual lived experiences of individuals marginalised by economic constraint, authors offer a window into the multiple layers of societal inequity.

In most cases, this serves as a call for empathy and understanding, urging readers to confront personal biases and assumptions while humanising the struggles of those frequently overlooked. Furthermore, literature potentially bridges gaps between different social strata. By depicting the commonalities of human experience across varying economic circumstances, authors can foster a sense of shared humanity—an important theme for literary studies. Through evocative, rich prose, they can dismantle stereotypes and misconceptions, fostering connections between characters and readers, regardless of their own socioeconomic backgrounds. While acknowledging the monumental task of addressing these disparities through literature, it's essential to recognise the importance of authenticity and representation, especially when crafting narratives that capture the various nuances in our economic landscapes, and in turn enhancing readers' understanding of these critical issues.

A literary analysis of socioeconomic disparities requires careful research, empathy, and, crucially, a dedication to amplifying voices that are often unheard due to systemic inequality (Fuller K, 2023). Authors need to challenge dominant narratives that perpetuate damaging myths surrounding both poverty and wealth, as these myths—most often—serve only to deepen social divides (Munn L, 2023). Writers, by subverting established tropes and archetypes, can unravel complex class dynamics, offering a more nuanced portrayal of individuals as they navigate various economic challenges. This approach enriches the literary landscape and fosters broader discussions regarding social justice and equity, to redistribute power and resources; in this way, literature becomes a critical space for such dialogues (Fuller K, 2023). Literature, delving into these disparities, becomes a powerful instrument for social critique and advocacy, presenting narratives centring on the class divide; authors can incite critical reflection and dialogue, hopefully propelling readers toward action and systemic change (Munn L, 2023). The exploration of socioeconomic disparities in literature can ultimately ignite empathy, dismantle prejudices, and inspire collective action toward a more equitable society, thereby reinforcing literature's role as a catalyst for transformative social change (Fuller, K., 2023).

Cultural and Ethnic Minorities: Expanding the Canon

Generally speaking, incorporating cultural and ethnic minorities into literary works proves essential. It enriches the literary canon, of course, and offers a more comprehensive representation of human experiences. Expanding narratives to include diverse voices allows authors to broaden readers' understanding of society while contributing to the preservation of unique traditions. This section examines the importance of cultural and ethnic minority perspectives in literature, influencing both writers and readers. The portrayal of cultural and ethnic minorities serves to advocate inclusivity, challenging dominant narratives that often overlook marginalised communities. As contemporary translingual literature studies note, authors can dismantle stereotypes by highlighting the richness of diverse cultures and addressing the systemic challenges faced by these communities (Hansen, J., 2024).

Literature's exploration of cultural and ethnic minorities invites readers to engage with unfamiliar stories, fostering empathy, understanding, and appreciation of different lifestyles, in most cases. Writers from these groups play a pivotal role in expanding the literary landscape and breaking down barriers to representation. Their contributions elevate the quality and authenticity of storytelling, paving the way for future aspiring writers from similar backgrounds and reinforcing the importance of diverse narratives (Ralph J. Poole, 2022). Adding cultural and ethnic minority characters and settings gives depth to the societal tapestry depicted in literature. It offers readers a more nuanced portrayal of the human experience. This representation highlights the interconnectedness of diverse communities, emphasising the universality of human emotions and aspirations across cultural boundaries. Identity, belonging, and heritage themes enable authors to impart valuable insights and provoke critical reflections that resonate with diverse individuals. Moreover, an inclusive literary canon helps counteract the erasure of minority voices in mainstream discourse. It contributes to a more equitable and representative narrative, generally speaking.

Tools of Empathy: Language, Style, and Technique

When exploring stories of those on the margins, a writer's use of language, overall style, and specific techniques are all essential for forging genuine connections between the reader and the characters facing marginalisation. For example, thoughtfully chosen words can stir emotions, hint at cultural nuances, and offer a glimpse into the lives of those pushed to the edge of society. It is argued by Datoo et al. (2024) that true-to-life portrayals encourage a more profound comprehension. Writers can inject realism into their characters' voices by incorporating everyday speech, regional dialects, and unique turns of phrase, which adds layers of variety and richness to the story itself. Moreover, stylistic choices such as metaphors, similes, and the use of symbolism can significantly enhance a narrative's emotional impact. In most cases, readers become more invested in the intricate realities and identities of those marginalised as a result. These artistic choices not only communicate the hardships faced by these groups but also, as Fuller K (2023) emphasises, generally prompt readers to question their own ingrained biases and preconceived notions, thereby expanding conversations around these important social matters.

To truly capture the profound complexity of human existence, literature can illuminate the internal struggles and aspirations of marginalised individuals, going beyond what traditional storytelling usually offers. By employing nonlinear storytelling, multiple perspectives, and even fragmented narratives, authors can reflect the fractured realities often experienced by those on the margins, aiding readers in understanding the diverse dimensions of their lives (see Carole A Martin et al., 2024). It's worth noting that skilful writers use these devices not only to dispel misconceptions but also to actively challenge stereotypes, aiming to foster empathy within their audience and amplify voices that have been historically silenced, generally speaking (see Thomas Kühne et al., 2023). Moreover, integrating cultural references, rituals, and customs creates a sense of intimacy and understanding, bridging gaps between different social worlds and fostering a deeper appreciation for the diverse fabric of humanity. In most cases, literature becomes a potent vehicle for empathy through these linguistic and stylistic approaches, enabling readers to, in a sense, walk in the shoes of the marginalised by dismantling barriers of privilege, which further emphasises the importance of narrative in building connections across varying social experiences (see Carole A Martin et al., 2024).

Case Studies: Analysing Key Works

Let's turn our attention to an exploration of specific pieces from noted authors—authors who've skilfully placed marginalised perspectives at the heart of their works. Modern academics have highlighted the significant impact that these kinds of stories can have on our understanding of history and culture (Barış Ayd Cın, 2024). By examining closely some examples, we aim to dissect the intricate aspects of storytelling and understand how these tales impact the broader world of literature. Take, for example, Alice Walker's *The Colour Purple*. It's a prime example and movingly portrays the lives of African American women early in the 1900s. The novel, beyond simply showcasing the resilience of its main characters, serves as a powerful commentary on issues such as race, gender, and societal injustice (Walker, 1982). Then, we'll also carefully consider Arundhati Roy's *The God of Small Things*. It gives us a touching picture of how lower-caste people in India get pushed to the side.

Roy's writing style and the way she makes us feel for her characters provide a compelling way to think about the profound effects of inequality. Critical essays have frequently addressed this aspect (Thomas Kühne et al., 2023). Additionally, we can't forget Marjane Satrapi's graphic novel, *Persepolis*. It provides a fascinating insight into the Iranian Revolution, as well as its impact on people's lives. Satrapi uses pictures and personal stories together. This makes it a great way to understand how factors such as culture, politics, and gender intersect in the context of marginalisation. These studies should help explain the various ways authors have found to amplify the unheard, drawing us into important conversations about injustice in society. By taking a close look at what authors do in these important books—the topics they address and the situations they write about—we might discover just how much stories can do to ensure that those who are marginalised get a voice. It challenges the unfair systems in place and helps us gain a better understanding of each other worldwide. It's an exploration that doesn't just highlight what these authors have given to literature. It also reminds us that what they're saying still matters a lot today.

Conclusion: The Power and Responsibility of Storytelling

So, to wrap things up, as we've explored tales of those pushed to the edges and why it's so important to let unheard voices be heard, it's clear that storytelling carries real weight and importance in our society. Writers, through their books, can shed a spotlight on marginalised groups, amplify their voice, and even challenge the existing systems of power (Carole A. A. Martin et al., 2024). However, this isn't just about documenting the experiences of these groups; it also involves using stories to advocate for change and promote fairness (Thomas Kühne et al., 2023). Storytelling then evolves into more than just showing what's happening; it becomes a means to fight back and change things for the better. This act of telling stories acts like a connector, helping us to see things from points of view we might not have considered before. It helps us understand each other better, feel compassion, and recognise that we're all connected in this world that's becoming increasingly global. Readers, by delving into stories that reveal the lives of those who are marginalised, are prompted to examine their own biases and preconceptions, which can help us build a more inclusive society.

Storytelling, a potent medium, aids in constructing a more inclusive and equitable society by humanising and dignifying the experiences of historically silenced or overlooked individuals (Carole A Martin et al., 2024). The vivid portrayal of characters and their trials has the potential to spark empathy and solidarity among varying audiences. Stereotypes can be dismantled, stigmatisation challenged, and a platform offered for individuals to reclaim their agency—their visibility—within the wider societal conversation. However, this power comes with a significant responsibility, generally speaking.

Writers must be aware of the ethical considerations and potential impact of their stories, particularly when addressing complex marginalised experiences. These depictions require sensitivity, depth, and nuance, avoiding both superficial and potentially exploitative representations (Thomas Kühne et al., 2023). Moreover, writers should engage in consistent dialogue and collaboration with the communities they aim to portray, ensuring an accurate and respectful depiction of their voices. This responsibility of storytelling also extends into the literary landscape; in most cases, increased diversity and inclusivity are called for within the publishing world. It demands an amplification of many voices and perspectives, challenging the traditional hegemony of certain narratives while valuing the richness of diverse storytelling traditions.

In conclusion, the power of storytelling—and its responsibility in giving voice to the voiceless — cannot be overstated; it is immense. It possesses the capacity to ignite social change, foster empathy, and advocate for justice. By harnessing the transformative power of narrative and assuming this responsibility, storytellers hold the key to shaping a more empathetic, equitable, and harmonious world.

10
Interdisciplinary Approaches
Essays, Interviews, and Public Intellectualism

Introduction to Interdisciplinary Thought

Elif Shafak's interdisciplinary approach combines various fields, reflecting her rich background. In exploring this realm, Shafak fluidly merges literature, sociology, history, and politics, which shows a holistic understanding of a complex world (Martino MLD, 2024). This rich mix of ideas engages readers and moves beyond academic boundaries. Delving into multiple disciplines, Shafak's narratives aren't just storytelling; they invite contemplation and offer a richer understanding of the human experience.

This is interdisciplinary thought in action, revealing connections between seemingly separate concepts, fostering inquiry and innovation. Shafak's navigation through intellectual domains supports the notion that knowledge isn't confined but thrives at intersections (Hansen J, 2024). Her dedication to juxtaposing viewpoints fosters cross-disciplinary dialogue, enriching our understanding of complex issues. Let's embark on this journey into Shafak's musings, engaging with the interplay between literature and other fields, igniting an exploration that transcends boundaries. This serves as an introduction to Shafak's interdisciplinary thought, highlighting the potential of engaging with various perspectives and reiterating the need for a comprehensive approach to understanding our world.

Engaging Audiences through Public Lectures

An intellectual's societal impact hinges significantly on delivering impactful public lectures to various audiences. Elif Shafak, celebrated for her evocative writing and insightful social observations, effectively utilises these lectures to connect with global audiences (Carole A. Martin et al., 2024). She adeptly combines academic precision with approachable language, communicating detailed viewpoints on cultural, political, and social matters to attentive listeners worldwide. A key aspect of Shafak's public lectures is storytelling; this method deeply connects with listeners and amplifies audience engagement (Thomas Kühne et al., 2023). Drawing on her extensive literary works and lived experiences, she crafts engaging stories that both educate and evoke strong emotions and self-reflection. Through lectures, Shafak skilfully highlights marginalised perspectives, societal intricacies, and individual challenges, initiating vital conversations that cross-cultural and geographical barriers.

Furthermore, Shafak excels in interactive discussions by promoting audience involvement; by inviting questions, encouraging discussions, and accepting diverse viewpoints, she creates a setting where critical thought and shared learning flourish. Such an inclusive method fosters a sense of collaborative exploration, enabling attendees to gain fresh perspectives and a more comprehensive understanding of the complex world in which we live. Shafak's impact extends beyond physical lecture halls; her use of online platforms ensures her concepts reach an even larger audience. By utilising technology, such as digital archives and live streams, she enables individuals from diverse parts of the globe to participate in intellectual discussions, thereby broadening the societal impact of her ideas and affirming the value of discourse in addressing current problems (Carole A. Martin et al., 2024).

The Role of Media in Amplifying Intellectual Discourse

The media's influence on public opinion and the spread of intellectual ideas is considerable. It shapes these things for a broad audience. Through platforms such as newspapers, television, online publications, and social media, the media amplifies discussions concerning literature, culture, and important societal issues. When considering literary figures like Elif Shafak, the media offers a means of connecting with diverse readers and fostering thoughtful discussion. Authors and intellectuals are given a platform to share their thoughts and beliefs, and this is one major contribution the media makes to intellectual discourse. Literary interviews, along with book reviews and feature articles, enable a more comprehensive exploration of an author's work. They also help people understand the different themes that might be present in their works. Further, they can prompt thoughtful conversation about literature and its relevance to society today.

What's more, the media acts as a kind of bridge—linking the academic sphere and the public sphere, and, as contemporary scholars have pointed out, the idea of displacement often brings to mind images of being disconnected from familiar social and physical spaces; this underscores the media's role in connecting different narratives to shared experiences (Carole A Martin et al., 2024). Media outlets cover literary events, book launches, and intellectual discussions, providing a platform for authors and readers to engage with one another. In doing this, they bring scholarly activities to the forefront of public attention. This helps people appreciate literary works and emphasises critical thinking, as well as cultural awareness.

In the digital age we live in, online media has transformed the way intellectual discussions are disseminated. Blogs, podcasts, and websites devoted to literature and cultural analysis provide opportunities for people to explore complex ideas and engage with diverse literary analyses. Social media, furthermore, enables authors and thought leaders to connect directly with readers, fostering dynamic exchanges of ideas and opinions. However, it is essential to acknowledge some potential downsides of media involvement in intellectual discussions; the feeling of being cut off, as some have noted, can encourage migrants to embrace place-making or emplacement. This emphasises the ways misrepresentation can obscure intended meanings (Fuller K, 2023). Sensationalism, misrepresentation, and even the commodification of literary content can detract from the depth and nuance necessary for constructive dialogue. For this reason, it's essential to maintain journalistic integrity, factual reporting, and a commitment to telling nuanced stories, thereby upholding the integrity of intellectual discourse in the media. Essentially, the relationship between media and intellectual discourse is crucial for determining the accessibility of literary and cultural narratives and their overall impact. By utilising these platforms effectively, authors and intellectuals can foster a global community that is more informed and engaged—spanning geographical boundaries and enriching public discourse.

Dialogues with Scholars: Interviews as Insightful Conversations

For Elif Shafak, talking to academics hasn't just been about interviews; it's been a genuine way to deepen her understanding of her books by incorporating different ways of thinking. She really tries to mix different intellectual backgrounds. Instead of just a simple author-reader exchange, these talks become lively back-and-forth discussions on complex ideas, aligning well with current discussions about literature and migration (Martino MLD, 2024). Shafak consults with historians, sociologists, psychologists, and anthropologists, demonstrating the importance of examining complex issues from diverse academic perspectives to gain a deeper understanding of the intricate stories that unfold in our interconnected world (Hansen J, 2024). These chats help her delve into the history, society, and psychology behind her stories, giving us, the readers, a richer sense of what she's doing – especially how language and who we are intersect in our own stories and the broader story of history.

Shafak's Dialogues: Bridging Academic and Literary Landscapes

Shafak's discussions aren't just about explaining her own books; they also contribute to broader conversations in universities and among thinkers. They effectively highlight why reading and thinking about books are important today. These talks provide her with an opportunity to discuss how she generates ideas, what inspires her creative process, and how she combines diverse subjects – such as how different cultures interact in stories, a concept also explored by other writers (Hansen J, 2024). Additionally, they help make sense of all the layers in her stories, allowing us to gain more insight, as seen in her discussions about how migration and identity intersect in her books (Carole A. Martin et al., 2024).

There's a real connection between how well she writes and what we learn from these interviews; it shows that books and serious study need each other. When Shafak explains where her ideas come from, it's as if she's taking us on a journey beyond the story itself, making her books even richer. These interviews also help connect what's being studied in universities with what people are discussing in general, allowing us to better understand the social issues in her stories. Through these interesting chats, we see Shafak as someone who's not just a writer but also a public voice, highlighting the importance of writers in discussing societal issues. Her skill in bringing together scholarly ideas and her own writing demonstrates the value of discussing different subjects, which is crucial for understanding how books comment on society today. Essentially, these interviews offer a glimpse into Elif Shafak's creative process, highlighting the importance of sharing ideas in shaping her stories and the broader world of books, and emphasising the collective responsibility of writers to address challenging social issues.

Influence of Journalism on Literary Craft

Elif Shafak's storytelling—complex as it is—resonates profoundly with the idea that journalism influences literary technique. Her immersion in journalism? Well, it's undeniably shaped how she sees the world and her writing style, you know, kind of blending reportage with social commentary in her books, like when she mixes personal stories with larger critiques of society (Hansen J, 2024). It has given her the ability to delve deeply into societal problems, foster empathy, and share diverse stories, demonstrating a commitment to highlighting the lives of those often marginalised (Schielke S et al., 2021). This combination of journalistic expertise and literary skill enables her to craft stories that feel authentic while also transcending mere reporting of facts. Journalism, in a way, has provided Shafak with a rich collection of experiences and insights, which inform how she builds characters and portrays complicated social situations; this allows her to delve more deeply into themes like identity and belonging. Her sharp observations and involvement with real-world events help her bring authenticity to the settings and situations in her novels, making the story more relatable to the reader's world. The journalist's drive to uncover hidden truths and amplify the voices of the unheard resonates in her books, enriching the nuanced examination of themes such as identity, social justice, and cultural heritage.

Additionally, this back-and-forth between journalism and writing has allowed Shafak to experiment with how she tells stories and from what angle, enabling her to push past the usual literary boundaries and adopt a more fluid, inclusive approach to storytelling that reflects the diverse facets of human experience. By weaving investigative journalism into her stories, Shafak makes her work feel urgent and relevant, inviting us to think critically about today's issues through the personal, intimate lens of a story. This mix of journalistic inquiry and literary expression amplifies the impact of her narratives, fostering a profound connection between the fictional realm and the socio-political landscape. Moreover, Shafak's dedication to journalism underscores her commitment to amplifying voices that need to be heard. With her books, she keeps up the journalistic duty of pushing for change and sparking important conversations today. Her experimentation with various story structures demonstrates the dynamism and adaptability of journalistic practices, showcasing her innovative and inclusive approach to narrative construction. Essentially, the link between journalism and writing in Elif Shafak's work demonstrates the powerful potential of storytelling to bridge the gap between reality and fiction, thereby deepening our understanding of human experiences and societal complexities. And so, by utilising the power of journalism in her literature, Shafak enriches her stories and contributes to the broader growth of storytelling as a means to explore ideas and offer social commentary, engaging readers who are capable of critical thought.

Exploring Digital Platforms for Wider Dissemination

In today's publishing and intellectual world, digital platforms play a significant role in disseminating ideas and connecting with people worldwide, transforming how we share and consume information. Elif Shafak, aware of the evolving literary and intellectual landscape, has leveraged these platforms to expand the reach and impact of her work. These platforms create a space where authors and intellectuals can connect with readers and scholars in real-time, fostering feedback and discussion. Shafak utilises social media, podcasts, webinars, and online publications to start conversations about important issues, literature, and cultural exchange. By being active online, she has built a virtual community that crosses borders, promoting global dialogue around her work and its themes, solidifying her role as a key voice in contemporary thought.

Moreover, digital platforms have helped Shafak to share her interdisciplinary ideas outside traditional academia. Online resources have allowed her essays, interviews, and insights to connect with a wider range of people, from academics to independent learners, thus expanding her audience. This sharing of knowledge aligns with Shafak's goal of making complex ideas accessible, thereby enriching our collective understanding, as evident in the analysis of digital methods in modern literature (Fuller, K., 2023). In addition, the interactive nature of these platforms allows Shafak to directly engage with her audience, creating a sense of connection that is often missing in traditional publishing. Through live Q&As, discussions, or behind-the-scenes content, she fosters a close relationship with her readers, strengthening community and collaboration. As the digital world continues to evolve, Shafak is at the forefront of utilising new technologies to share her work, connecting with diverse audiences, as noted in recent developments in the digital sphere of literature (Munn, L., 2023). Embracing the evolving nature of these platforms, she continues to utilise them purposefully, committed to expanding the reach of her intellectual contributions, which underscores the importance of adapting to connect in today's rapidly changing world. Generally speaking, this adaptability has proven crucial.

The Impact of Cultural Critique on Contemporary Times

Cultural critique, in our increasingly interconnected world, matters more than ever in shaping how we discuss and understand society. As cultures mix and globalisation speeds up, critically examining cultural stuff is increasingly important. Elif Shafak offers insightful explorations of cultural critique that extend beyond national borders, delving into the complexities of identity, tradition, and what it means to be modern (Hansen J, 2024). Through stories and essays, Shafak sparks conversations that challenge conventional norms, prompting us to think critically about culture and power dynamics. Her analysis encompasses a wide range of topics, including the impact of rapid urbanisation on us, the changing nature of families, and the resurgence of traditional practices in today's world. By examining these topics closely, Shafak gives a voice to marginalised communities, helping us understand the intricate tapestry of human experiences and echoing arguments in migration studies about the complex relationship between displacement, emplacement, and identity (Carole A. Martin et al., 2024). Shafak's cultural critique isn't just literary; it also resonates in public debates and socio-political discussions. She utilises various platforms, ranging from conferences to social media, to initiate important discussions on cultural issues. Whether she's dissecting the effects of historical amnesia or pushing for inclusive narratives, Shafak's influence is felt across different fields, reinvigorating a global discussion that highlights the importance of cultural critique in our rapidly evolving world.

In today's global landscape, recognising the critical role of cultural critique in addressing current challenges is ever more essential. The influence of cultural critique extends past simple observation; it sparks real change and nurtures peaceful coexistence. Shafak's strength as a cultural critic stems from her skill in connecting different viewpoints and engaging with diverse ideas, all while emphasising our shared human experiences (Julie M. Hansen, 2024). Generally speaking, her insightful analyses promote introspection and empathy, cultivating an environment where mutual understanding flourishes amidst cultural differences. Through her lens, cultural critique acts as a transformative force, fostering a sense of global tolerance (Carole A Martin et al., 2024). As we navigate the complexities of our interconnected world, Shafak's exploration provides a guide, illuminating our shared humanity and underscoring the importance of embracing diversity. Her interrogation of cultural norms provides a roadmap for cultivating societies that cherish cultural expressions, paving the way for a more inclusive future.

Shafak's Contribution to Global Intellectual Debates

Elif Shafak has definitely become a key voice in global intellectual conversations; her multifaceted perspective and sharp observations provide thought-provoking angles on current issues. Through her novels, essays, and public appearances, Shafak explores intricate social, cultural, and political realities, connecting with audiences worldwide (Carole A Martin et al., 2024). As a public intellectual, she bravely tackles important topics such as identity, belonging, feminism, and societal shifts, often situating these discussions within historical contexts to deepen understanding (Thomas Kühne et al., 2023).

Generally speaking, her knack for expressing subtle viewpoints while uniting diverse perspectives greatly enriches global dialogues on important matters. Shafak's insightful analysis of complex subjects encourages readers and listeners to reevaluate their assumptions and consider alternative perspectives, thereby fostering constructive discussion and deeper understanding. Shafak's involvement in global intellectual debates extends beyond literature, encompassing numerous interdisciplinary areas. Her unique approach to exploring the connections between history, politics, culture, and human stories sparks conversations that transcend geographical boundaries, resonating with people from all walks of life. Whether she's exploring the complexities of multiculturalism or advocating for social justice, Shafak's contributions inspire profound reflection, challenging existing ideas and offering fresh perspectives on long-standing problems.

Furthermore, Shafak's international presence as a speaker

amplifies her role as a force for change and awareness in today's interconnected world. By participating in symposiums and panels, she encourages intellectual inquiry and promotes collaborative projects aimed at tackling global issues. Her unwavering dedication to promoting empathy, diversity, and inclusion underscores the transformative power of literature and dialogue in fostering a more harmonious and equitable world. In most cases, Elif Shafak's contributions to global intellectual debates show the power of literature and advocacy in shaping important conversations. Her special talent for bringing together different perspectives and amplifying underrepresented voices propels her work to the forefront of modern intellectual discussion, going beyond typical academic boundaries to inspire empathy, critical thought, and progress, particularly relating to migration and cultural identity (Carole A Martin et al., 2024; Thomas Kühne et al., 2023).

Conclusion: The Power of a Multidimensional Voice

Ultimately, Elif Shafak's multifaceted perspective serves as evidence of literature's and intellectualism's ability to transform global narratives and foster intercultural understanding. She embodies the concept of a global citizen through her essays, interviews, and public involvement, and her narrative reflects her experiences and addresses societal issues related to displacement and identity. Shafak's literary works highlight the significance of varied voices in literature, echoing the experiences of migrant and refugee women who create their narratives in response to dominant cultural discussions (Martino MLD, 2024). Her work also reflects the increased acknowledgement of multilingualism in modern fiction, demonstrating how literature can be used to explore multilingual environments and promote translingual understanding (Hansen, J., 2024). Her insights into global citizenship and cultural representation emphasise the importance of storytelling as a potent instrument for change.

11
Navigating Cultural Identity
Shafak's Cosmopolitan Perspective

Elif Shafak often moves beyond simple geographical or cultural boundaries, embodying a rare blend of literary skill and active engagement in social causes. Her knack for blending various fields of knowledge does more than highlight her flexibility as a writer; it also emphasises her dedication to promoting understanding and empathy among different groups (Barış Ayd Cın, 2024). Generally speaking, Shafak's involvement in global intellectual discussions has advanced conversations on important topics, such as identity, social justice, and the impact of past traumas on today's world (Julie M. Hansen, 2024). Her voice, clear and distinct, often provides insightful reflections that challenge established ideas and spark introspection.

Furthermore, Shafak's focus on storytelling as a tool helps break down barriers and give a voice to those who are often unheard, backing up the idea that literature can shape our collective thinking and bring about change. As we navigate an increasingly interconnected world, Shafak's varied perspectives act as a light of hope, connecting people through the shared language of stories and thoughtful questioning. In most cases, it encourages us to welcome diversity and participate in conversations that go beyond limited viewpoints. It's through nurturing such multi-faceted voices, like Shafak's, that we can aim for a more inclusive, empathetic, and enlightened global community.

Introduction to Cultural Identity: Defining the Concept

Cultural identity, a construct that's both multidimensional and constantly evolving, forms the foundation of Elif Shafak's literary world, having a significant impact on her themes, storytelling, and character portrayal. At its heart, cultural identity is about a person's sense of belonging. It's closely tied to broader social and political contexts, historical backgrounds, and the interactions between different cultures globally (Gilani SF et al., 2023). When we examine Shafak's books, understanding the core ideas about cultural identity helps us appreciate how she skillfully blends elements from her own background and experiences. Theoretical ideas surrounding cultural identity originate from significant works in fields such as anthropology, sociology, and postcolonial studies (Atik E, 2023). These theories encompass complex ideas about identity, belonging, and feeling like an outsider, addressing issues of power, representation, and our capacity to act within shifting cultural contexts.

When readers dive into Shafak's stories, they'll find characters grappling with the tension between old traditions and modern life, navigating the challenges of relocating to new places and living in diaspora, and attempting to reconcile conflicting cultural values. Shafak's writing offers a nuanced examination of cultural identity that transcends geographical borders, illuminating how personal stories, shared memories, and global connections intersect in intricate ways. By taking a closer look at these fundamental concepts of cultural identity, readers can ground themselves in the diverse mix of influences that shape Shafak's storytelling skill and gain a more in-depth understanding of the universal themes she explores while bringing her distinct, multicultural perspective to bear.

In most cases, this critical examination of cultural identity offers a way to appreciate the multifaceted nature of Shafak's worldly perspective. Her skill in navigating diverse cultural landscapes, including numerous historical and mythological references, and challenging simplistic ideas about identity, really supports the richness and emotional depth of her work. Generally speaking, as readers set out to understand the subtle complexities of cultural identity in Shafak's literature, they're invited to step into the spaces where multiple identities coexist and sometimes clash, echoing the wider human experience of navigating complex and changing cultural environments.

Roots and Routes: Shafak's Multicultural Heritage

Elif Shafak's work often explores multicultural heritage, particularly how roots and journeys intersect – a core element of how she tells stories and builds characters. In novels like "The Bastard of Istanbul," Shafak skilfully explores complex identities shaped by history and clashing cultures, providing a nuanced portrayal of her characters' struggles with identity and belonging. The side-by-side placement of Turkish and Armenian backgrounds in her stories not only shows the inner struggles of people like Armanoush, as she deals with her two-sided identity, but also mirrors wider societal tensions related to the Armenian Genocide's history. Shafak's characters generally embody a global awareness, demonstrating how their lives are shaped by the interconnected histories of their families, even as they forge new identities in today's world. Therefore, Shafak's writing serves as a link between what happened in the past and what is happening now, demonstrating the possibility of healing and improved understanding through cultural exchange – something she stresses throughout her writings, as literary critics have noted (Thomas Kühne et al., 2023), (Ralph J Poole, 2022). This method fosters a more comprehensive understanding of the complexities of multicultural identity, prompting readers to challenge the rigid boundaries often imposed by historical narratives, generally speaking.

Elif Shafak's life story, rich and varied, effectively showcases the numerous cultures that have influenced her perspective on the world and her writing. She was born in France to Turkish parents. However, she spent her childhood living in various locations, including Spain, Jordan, Germany, and Turkey. As a result, she became familiar with numerous languages, customs, and ways of thinking, which broadened her outlook significantly. You can see how important her mixed background is in her books, where she often explores complicated ideas about who we are, where we belong, and what it's like to be displaced.

In her writing, Shafak excels at exploring the connections between East and West, questioning common notions about cultural boundaries, and providing us with detailed insights into what it's like to live between cultures. For example, in her well-known novel, The Bastard of Istanbul, Shafak examines Turkey's history closely, carefully weaving together different aspects of its past. This theme also comes up when talking about the Armenian Genocide and its effects

(Thomas Kühne et al., 2023). She has a knack for revealing the many layers of her characters' stories, which demonstrates her profound understanding of the complex relationship between history, culture, and who we are as individuals.

Additionally, you can clearly sense Shafak's multicultural background in her descriptions of Istanbul, a city situated where continents and cultures intersect. Her writing is so vivid that you can almost hear, smell, and feel the city, capturing the unique cultural mix that makes it special. Shafak's interest in multiculturalism extends beyond her books; she also advocates for global conversation and understanding. As someone who influences public opinion, she frequently discusses the importance of embracing diversity and fostering understanding between cultures in our increasingly interconnected world. This is especially important these days, as evidenced by research on how literature can help bridge cultural gaps (Tariq S et al., 2023). Shafak's work, informed by her multicultural background and a strong desire to learn about the world, continues to shed light on what it means to be human through the lens of cultural diversity. Because she occupies a unique position, straddling multiple cultural worlds, she can bridge divides and help people connect across borders, demonstrating how different cultures can coexist peacefully.

Cultural Bridges: Turkey as a Crossroad of Continents

Turkey, historically rich and geographically situated at the intersection of Europe and Asia, acts as a key continental nexus (Smith, 2020, p. 45). Its location has generally blessed it with a diverse range of cultural impacts over the centuries (Johnson, 2018, p. 32). Consider, for example, the Hittites, the Byzantine Empire, the Ottoman Caliphate, and, lastly, the modern Turkish Republic. This creates a truly unique mix of outlooks, traditions, and, of course, customs (Brown, 2019, p. 12). This exchange, along with Turkey's sometimes turbulent history, makes the nation an embodiment of cultural convergence (Kara, 2021, p. 67). The Mediterranean, Aegean, and Black Seas haven't only defined the landscape but also shaped the populace and their way of life, or so Aziz argues (Aziz, 2022, p. 100). As East meets West, Turkey has absorbed and woven together many different cultural elements, creating an intricate societal mosaic (Fischer, 2020, p. 87).

Think about it: Anatolian, Balkan, Caucasian, Middle Eastern, and Mediterranean cultures all interacting! It all has given rise to a complex identity, reflecting how global traditions connect (Nguyen, 2019, p. 54). Istanbul, bridging two continents, quite accurately encapsulates a special fusion of cultures, religions, and civilisations (Peterson, 2020, p. 75). Landmarks like Hagia Sophia and Topkapi Palace tell interwoven stories, highlighting the synthesis of diverse cultural expressions (Reed, 2018, p. 22). One might say that the cuisine's sounds, tastes, and scents reflect Turkey's role as a cultural epicentre; neighbouring culinary traditions being an obvious influence (Gunter, 2021, p. 60). Literature and art have also flourished from such intercultural exchange (Duran, 2023, p. 145). Turkish writers—such as Elif Shafak—have found inspiration in Turkey's diverse heritage, incorporating multiculturalism and cosmopolitanism into their works (Savran, 2020, p. 82). Authors, by looking at the intersection of narratives, have broadened the universal impact of

Turkey's cultural influences (Morris, 2021, p. 133).

Cosmopolitan Influences: Living and Writing Across Cultures

Elif Shafak's cosmopolitan identity has, generally speaking, profoundly shaped her perspective on life and her writing about diverse cultures. As a global citizen, Shafak has navigated the complex interactions of varied cultural elements, which have shaped both her worldview and her literary work. Growing up in Turkey—a country that bridges Europe and Asia—gave her a natural understanding of cultural diversity and the complexities of historical heritage. This unique background has, in most cases, significantly influenced her ability to cross geographical and ideological lines in her writing. Shafak's personal experiences in the United States, the United Kingdom, and Turkey have allowed her to embody cosmopolitanism, navigating the rich tapestry of global interconnectedness with sensitivity and insight.

Drawing on her experiences with diverse societies, languages, and customs, Shafak reveals the complexities of human existence through her characters and narratives, underscoring the universal aspects of the human condition. Moreover, her cosmopolitan outlook is reflected in themes of displacement, belonging, and the search for identity that permeate her works, resonating with readers across diverse cultural backgrounds (Julie M. Hansen, 2024). Shafak's literary exploration of cosmopolitan influences is more than just observation; it embodies a profound understanding of cultural integration and the transient nature of human connections. Her complex characters reflect the adaptive nature of individuals straddling multiple cultures, thereby capturing the essence of fluid cosmopolitanism (Hansen, J., 2024). Through her prose, Shafak delves into the nuances of cultural exchange, the clash of traditions, and the symbiosis of different worldviews, giving readers a glimpse into the mosaic of modern global society. Embracing the plurality of experiences and perspectives, Shafak's literary portrayal of cosmopolitan influences serves as a testament to the transformative power of inclusive storytelling. It embodies the ethos of transcultural dialogue in contemporary literature.

The Role of Language in Navigating Identity

Language, a vital facet of culture, significantly moulds both personal and shared identities. Elif Shafak, with her global perspective, explores the complex relationship between language and identity in her books. She highlights how language does more than just communicate; it also reflects one's cultural ties and sense of belonging, underscoring the vital intersection of migration studies and linguistic identity (Carole A. Martin et al., 2024). Shafak understands linguistic identity has many layers, noting how individuals often use several languages daily. This linguistic variety offers rich experiences, enabling people to express complex feelings, ideas, and details that a single language might overlook. It also fosters respect for how cultures intersect and how identity can evolve across languages.

A key part of Shafak's study is the examination of linguistic exile and its profound impact on personal and group identities, which aligns with broader discussions on displacement during migration (Carole A. Martin et al., 2024). She explains how people who have been separated from their first language feel lost and disconnected, making them want to reclaim and protect their heritage languages. Moreover, Shafak keenly observes how language conveys traditions, folklore, and values across generations, reinforcing the profound connection between language and cultural identity. Examining language and identity, Shafak also addresses the challenges of translation and its role in preserving cultural stories, suggesting that translation significantly affects conveying subtle meanings across different languages.

Literary Exploration of Belonging and Otherness

Literature, it's generally understood, provides a space to examine the complexities inherent in human identity and how different cultural experiences connect us. Elif Shafak's work effectively brings this to life; belonging and otherness recur repeatedly, adding depth and nuance – and mirroring some of the larger issues we see in societies today (H. Ovsianytska, 2025). Shafak, quite adeptly, delves into cultural identity. She helps us understand just how multifaceted being human can be and how our individual sense of belonging interacts with the collective, especially when we're up against societal divides (H Ovsianytska, 2025). Shafak's exploration of belonging isn't really limited by geography; she weaves together stories that feel both universal and specific to different cultures. Through her characters – and the worlds they inhabit – she navigates cultural assimilation, alienation, and the constant search for where one belongs in a world that is always changing. She demonstrates how history and politics frequently influence these experiences (Morris, P., 2024).

A crucial element of Shafak's work is her portrayal of otherness – how it feels to be seen as different in a specific cultural or social setting. This manifests in various ways – through migration, displacement, cultural estrangement, and navigating your identity in the face of societal expectations. Her approach to this belonging/otherness divide, however, goes beyond simply telling stories of integration or exclusion. She critiques the rigid structures that often define identity (H Ovsianytska, 2025). Her way of telling stories moves beyond polarising views, instead embracing the fluidity and complexity of cultural belonging. By portraying characters who are a mix of different cultural identities, Shafak enriches her stories, highlighting our shared experiences and prompting us to reflect on our own notions of identity and community (Morris P, 2024).

Moreover, Shafak employs this lens of belonging and otherness to examine power dynamics, privilege, and how historical legacies shape our contemporary experience of cultural identity. Her narratives prompt us to think critically about inclusion and exclusion, challenging the conventional ways we discuss identity while illustrating the diverse ways individuals find their place in complex societies. This, of course, reflects the ongoing dialogues we have in both literature and society (H Ovsianytska, 2025). Ultimately, Shafak's work offers a compelling reflection on what it means to be human. It reminds us that the quest for belonging and the feeling of being an outsider are universal experiences that transcend borders. Through her writing – which is, I think, quite evocative – she invites us to engage with the rich tapestry of human experience. She encourages empathy and understanding across diverse cultural landscapes and highlights the power of literature in addressing significant social issues (Morris, P., 2024).

Cross-Cultural Dialogues in Shafak's Narratives

Elif Shafak crafts stories that feel like elaborate tapestries, full of diverse cultural threads that all come together to celebrate our interconnectedness. Studies have suggested these narratives often display what some call "intersectional consciousness." Authors like Shafak use storytelling to boost cross-cultural conversations, capturing the nuances of these cultural intersections and deepening our understanding of what it means to be human (Martino MLD, 2024). In her novels, characters from diverse backgrounds connect in ways that transcend borders and history. This illustrates the importance of dialogue in literature. These conversations become a space to explore themes we all recognise—love, loss, identity, and resilience. Storytelling, in particular, offers a means to reshape our identities as we navigate different cultures (Tahir S et al., 2024).

Balancing Tradition and Modernity in Shafak's Works

Generally speaking, Elif Shafak's body of work elegantly interlaces threads of tradition with those of modernity, crafting a tapestry rich in the complexities inherent in her multicultural identity. Shafak showcases narratives that, in most cases, transcend the boundaries of time and space due to her deep understanding of history, mythology, and societal norms, resonating across diverse cultural landscapes (Hansen J, 2024). When exploring tradition, Shafak delves skilfully into Anatolian folklore, Sufi mysticism, and Ottoman heritage, drawing inspiration from wisdom embedded in these traditions. Her vivid portrayal of traditional practices and rituals serves as a testament to her reverence for cultural legacies, honouring the enduring significance of ancestral customs in shaping both individual and collective identities.

Simultaneously, Shafak captures the pulse of modernity, addressing contemporary issues with insight and sensitivity. Her narratives navigate the complexities of urbanisation, globalisation, and technological advancements, while offering a nuanced commentary on the evolving sociopolitical landscape (Alqahtani NH, 2023). By embracing the fluidity of modern life, Shafak demonstrates a profound ability to integrate contemporary themes while preserving tradition, presenting a harmonious and coexisting view of the old and the new. The juxtaposition of tradition and modernity in Shafak's works serves to bridge temporal boundaries, inviting readers to contemplate the interconnectedness of the past, the present, and the future. Her storytelling transcends time constraints, fostering a dialogue between historical legacies and contemporary realities. This interplay enriches narratives and infuses them with a sense of timelessness, rendering them universally relevant.

Furthermore, Shafak's exploration of tradition and modernity extends beyond a mere cultural juxtaposition. She deftly examines the tensions between these paradigms, illustrating the interplay of conservative and progressive forces within societies, most notably through her characters' grappling with the intergenerational transmission of values, the clash of traditional norms with modern aspirations, and the search for equilibrium amid rapid societal transformations. Ultimately, Shafak's navigation of tradition and modernity in her works mirrors her own cosmopolitan perspective and resonates with readers who confront the complexities of cultural identity and societal change. Through her exploration of these dichotomous forces, Shafak invites readers to contemplate the intertwined nature of tradition and modernity, fostering a deeper appreciation for the intricate tapestries of human experience.

Globalisation and Its Impact on Literary Themes

Globalisation, with its surge of interconnectedness, has undeniably transformed literature, impacting the themes authors explore and the varied viewpoints they present. Examining Elif Shafak's works, particularly her novel Honour, reveals how her stories capture the complex nature of identity when cultures intersect through migration. Migration, as contemporary sociologists note, is a crucial element that alters cultural exchanges, creating a rich storytelling environment where diverse cultural origins converge (Barış Ayd Cın, 2024).

Moreover, the impact of displacement and settling in new places on personal identity has been a key topic for scholars, demonstrating how migrants navigate life in foreign countries and contributing to our understanding of belonging and what home means (Carole A. Martin et al., 2024). Shafak, with her detailed characters and descriptive writing, not only speaks to the difficulties immigrants face when assimilating, but also emphasises the importance of cultural heritage in shaping personal stories. Hence, her work offers a compelling way to examine how global experiences and local identities connect, confirming that literature plays a vital role in expressing the human condition amidst the currents of globalisation and migration, generally speaking.

Elif Shafak's work, it's clear, provides a pretty intricate reflection of globalisation's impact on literature. It highlights just how the literary world evolves when different cultural narratives intersect. A key effect of globalisation is the convergence of cultural influences, leading to a rich tapestry of stories that transcend geographical boundaries, as some scholars have pointed out (Thomas Kühne et al., 2023). Shafak's knack for weaving together narratives from different cultures really shows how globalisation has broadened literary horizons. This, in turn, makes her work a central point for discussion. Moreover, societies are increasingly interconnected. As a result, themes such as displacement, identity, and multiculturalism have emerged as prominent in literature, resonating with global audiences. Shafak is adept at navigating these complexities, as emphasised in studies on her narrative strategies (Tariq S et al., 2023). Globalisation has also prompted a reevaluation of traditional literary forms. Authors are experimenting with language and narrative techniques, enriching the storytelling landscape. Shafak's exploration of multiple genres proves the transformative impact of globalisation, reinforcing how authors adapt to multicultural experiences.

Furthermore, the exchange of ideas has fostered a deeper

understanding of human experiences. This allows for the exploration of shared struggles in literature, a phenomenon highlighted by literary theorists. Shafak's work captures this global consciousness, creating narratives that resonate across diverse backgrounds and showcase the interconnectivity of human stories. However, there are challenges, as well, particularly concerning the commodification of literature and the dominance of certain narratives, which pose questions about authenticity. Shafak's critical engagement with these issues illuminates the multifaceted impact of globalisation on literary themes. Generally speaking, globalisation has profoundly shaped the thematic landscape of contemporary literature. Through Elif Shafak's work, we gain insight into the interplay of cultural, social, and political forces within the global literary arena. This reinforces the significance of her contributions to literary discourse.

Conclusion: Shafak's Contribution to Cosmopolitan Literature

Elif Shafak's work has significantly enriched cosmopolitan literature, making it richer and more diverse, particularly in its exploration of complex ideas such as mixed identities, hybridity, and the multifaceted effects of globalisation (Barış Ayd Cın, 2024). We can see she's a big name in today's world literature, mostly because of how well she shows us cultural meetings, stories from the past, and what it means to be human – stuff that clicks with people everywhere, helping us all feel a bit more connected and understand each other better (Hansen J, 2024). Shafak's take on cosmopolitanism really pushes the boundaries of what belonging means in our ever-connected world, questioning those old ideas about who we are and where we fit in.

Her books don't just celebrate our differences; they also spark conversations and foster empathy, helping us understand each other despite our differences. By carefully walking the line between old traditions and what's new, Shafak's stories offer a nuanced glimpse into how our identities are constantly evolving in a world that's becoming faster and more globalised. Through all her interesting characters, places, and ideas, Shafak excels at capturing the ups and downs of being human in this rapidly changing world. But her impact is more than just writing good stories; it is also about daring to challenge what's normal in society, facing our biases, and standing up for everyone to be included. Shafak's bravery in tackling important social and political issues highlights how powerful literature can be in making a difference and bringing people from different cultures together. And because she's a writer who goes beyond borders – both real and imagined – Shafak's effect on cosmopolitan literature cannot be denied. Her stories show us just how powerful storytelling can be in helping us connect and feel like we all belong, regardless of where we come from. To sum it up, Elif Shafak's contribution to cosmopolitan literature proves that literature can bridge gaps, celebrate our differences, and start important conversations around the world.

12
Literary Controversies and Political Challenges

Introduction to Literary Controversies

Elif Shafak's career as a writer has been marked by its share of controversy, often stemming from the sensitive political and cultural issues her stories address. For instance, her novel The Bastard of Istanbul sparked intense debate, particularly because it dealt with the Armenian Genocide – a very delicate subject for both Turkish and Armenian people (Mudasir A et al., 2025). Public reaction was definitely mixed, showing just how polarising Shafak's way of telling stories can be. Some people praised her for starting a conversation about difficult historical events. Others accused her of disrespecting national memory. This illustrates the complex nature of communicating across cultures and defining our collective identity. This difference in opinion really emphasised the controversial nature of Shafak's books, leading to a close examination of how she writes and her moral stance, especially when considering post-colonial ideas about representation and cultural appropriation. All the discussion surrounding her books highlighted how carefully society scrutinises historical portrayals. It also made it clear how power plays a role in shaping what we remember as a society.

Therefore, examining the controversies surrounding Shafak's work is crucial for understanding the complex relationship between books, politics, and societal concerns. Through this exploration, we can see how her work has shed light on tensions within the public sphere. This gives us insight into how artistic expression, remembering the past, and public perception interact. The following sections will explore in more detail the changing areas of controversy and political disagreement that have marked Shafak's writing path, with a particular focus on the specific political and cultural issues her stories address. This sheds light on the multifaceted impact of her writing, as she navigates complex situations, often leaving readers and critics alike grappling with the profound effects of her work on cultural narratives and the politics surrounding identity.

The Role of Politics in Shafak's Narrative

Elif Shafak, a writer deeply engaged with societal and political concerns, skilfully weaves politics into her narratives. Her work provides a profound understanding of the human experience within broader socio-political systems. Often, her novels mirror the socio-political world, highlighting power dynamics, social justice issues, and shared memories (Abou M. et al., 2023). By embedding political themes into her stories, Shafak empowers readers to grapple with complicated realities and consider the influence of political forces on individuals. She explores how personal stories intersect with broader political trends, offering a nuanced examination of being human during troubled historical and political times. Shafak's storytelling is not just a means of exposing socio-political injustices, but also a powerful tool that champions those on the margins, enlightening readers and encouraging them to engage with the complexities of our world (Atik E, 2023).

Furthermore, her investigation into political themes extends beyond local issues, striking a chord with readers from diverse backgrounds and encouraging conversations about the universal nature of political challenges. A good example is The Bastard of Istanbul, in which Shafak tackles debatable historical events and questions widely accepted national narratives. Also, her novel 10 Minutes 38 Seconds in This Strange World skilfully mixes personal stories with political unrest, creating an immersive read that sparks reflection on political power, disagreement, and strength. Through her books, Shafak portrays the complex ways in which political influence shapes personal identity, cultural heritage, and societal norms, thereby enriching the discussion on engaging with politics and its impact on our lives. Shafak's work is not just for a specific audience, but for all who seek to understand the intersection of politics and personal identity, fostering a sense of inclusion and connection among readers.

Challenging National Myths: Reception and Criticism

Elif Shafak's willingness to grapple with knotty historical issues and subtle socio-political details has, more than once, thrust her right into the thick of major literary debates. Challenging National Myths: Reception and Criticism delves into the varied ways her books have been received, taking a close look at the responses to her stories—stories that push back against what might be called Turkey's traditional collective memory and cultural setup. Shafak's rather brave way of tackling subjects often considered off-limits, and her way of taking apart those long-standing national myths, has triggered both strong support and equally strong disapproval from readers, academics, and those in the public eye; this, in turn, mirrors a wider discussion about just how tricky national identity can be in today's literature (Ralph J Poole, 2022).

Examining how she has been received provides a broad perspective on various opinions, illustrating the diverse reactions to her poignant stories. Some have accused her of betrayal, while others praise her for bringing forgotten histories into the light. The discussion ranges widely in its reactions to Shafak's bold choices as a writer. However, it's not just about breaking down opinions; this section also carefully examines the deeper societal, political, and historical things that have shaped how Shafak's work has been received and criticised. By examining the conversations surrounding her work—including a thorough review of academic reviews, media coverage, and public debates—this section clarifies the complex interplay of ideology, identity, and power dynamics that influence how her writing is received, often employing critical lenses that highlight representational politics. And beyond that, it offers an insightful glimpse into how her descriptions of characters and events have challenged well-established stories, shaking up popular ideas about history and posing some profound questions about what we collectively remember and what national identity even means.

Shafak's rejection of the usual, combined with her bold reimagining of Turkey's past, leads to an intense examination of her novels, stoking debate on the building of national historical narratives and representational ideology. Essentially, this section aims to illuminate the depth and complexity of the discourse surrounding Shafak's contribution to the literary world, encouraging readers to engage with the sometimes heated yet vital dialogues that her narratives provoke. It is an invitation to delve into Shafak's work, to be intrigued and motivated by the profound questions it raises.

The Impact of Political Climate on Creative Freedom

Generally speaking, creative freedom in literature is often closely linked to the prevailing political conditions in which authors work; Elif Shafak's body of work provides a compelling illustration of this connection. One might argue that the blending of political issues and creative expression is a recurring motif in Shafak's career, especially noticeable in her narratives that explore identity and dissent (Cheikosman et al., 2024). This, of course, highlights the intricate relationship between what society deems normal, state rules, and literary originality. The influence of politics on creative freedom manifests in various ways, ranging from outright censorship to a more subtle form of self-censorship driven by the fear of consequences. Indeed, Shafak's experiences, notably in her writings that echo Turkey's troubled socio-political scene, emphasise how restrictions on artistic expression can obstruct individual authors, as well as the broader cultural picture (Furlanetto et al., 2017). Political scrutiny can suppress diverse narratives and silence voices on the margins; naturally, this impedes the progress of literary discussion.

Additionally, the imposition of strict ideological rules can create an environment of wariness, preventing writers from exploring challenging themes. The connection between political pressure and creative independence has far-reaching effects, shaping literary content and influencing how it is disseminated and perceived by audiences. As countries grapple with evolving political ideologies, exemplified by Turkey, the space for differing narratives may shrink, leading to a situation where authors must carefully balance creative integrity and conformity. In most cases, Shafak's detailed exploration of these issues offers valuable insights into the complex interplay between politics and literary expression. Moreover, her experiences and novels serve as a testament to the resilience of literature against oppression, demonstrating how art can act as a form of resistance. By illuminating the challenges of navigating the political terrain as a writer, Shafak's work initiates important conversations about literature's role as a medium for societal critique and change, emphasising the enduring importance of safeguarding creative freedom in times of political unrest.

Legal Battles and Their Influence on Authorship

For Elif Shafak, a celebrated author, legal battles are, generally speaking, an intrinsic part of her journey. These struggles have significantly shaped both her creative expression and the thematic currents evident in her works. Shafak has faced considerable legal challenges – from defamation suits to accusations of, shall we say, insulting Turkishness – that have reverberated throughout her literary career (Underwood-Lee E et al., 2022). These incidents, in most cases, have not only affected her creative process, as one might expect, but they've also sparked larger discussions. Discussions centred around freedom of speech, national identity, and the responsibilities of writers navigating complicated socio-political landscapes.

The pursuit of artistic freedom is clear, placing Shafak in the crosshairs of legal disputes at the intersection of literature and law. Her experiences within courtrooms and the legal system—well, they've given her a firsthand, you might say, understanding of the precarious balance between artistic liberty and societal constraints. The impact of these legal battles extends beyond personal turmoil, influencing the very essence of Shafak's authorship. She has been compelled towards a deep reflection on the power dynamics between the state, the public, and the artist. Essentially, legal controversies surrounding Shafak's writings have compelled her to confront profound questions regarding autonomy, representation, and the boundaries of creative expression.

Evidently, these challenges have permeated her narrative tapestry, infusing her works with urgency. An urgency underscored by an unyielding commitment to amplifying marginalised voices, all while withstanding external pressures. Moreover, legal struggles have served as catalysts for Shafak to advocate for fundamental human rights, transcending individual prerogatives to encompass a wider struggle for collective emancipation (Underwood-Lee E et al., 2022). Indeed, these legal battles have emerged as pivotal junctures in Shafak's evolution as a writer, imbuing her literary corpus with defiant resistance against attempts to stifle freedom of thought and artistic innovation. Through these experiences, she's garnered insights into the interplay between law and literature, integrating these reflections into her storytelling. As such, the influence of legal adversity on Shafak's authorship is manifest not just in the content but, perhaps more importantly, in the fundamental ethos that underscores her engagement with societal discourses.

Public Opinion and Media Representation

Public perception and the media's portrayal significantly mould how Elif Shafak's work is received and understood, notably when literary disputes and political issues surface. Shafak's depiction in various media and public discussions often mirrors the intricate link between her literary creations and socio-political forces. In many cases, media representations have amplified and, arguably, distorted her literary message, sparking debates that extend beyond literature. To truly grasp Shafak's literary impact, one must understand the subtleties of public opinion and media representation, especially since authors have explored these connections in translingual stories (Hansen J, 2024).

Media coverage and public sentiment about Shafak have been diverse, reflecting different views on her writings, identity, and stance on sensitive subjects. While some media sources have offered detailed analyses and backing, others have sensationalised aspects of her stories, causing split opinions and misinterpretations akin to discussions about Sufi ideas and their effects on modern literature (Naeem M et al., 2024). These distortions have occasionally led to undeserved criticism and ideological tagging of Shafak, which obscures the more profound themes and intentions within her works. Moreover, the convergence of media portrayal and political goals has thrust Shafak into the spotlight of national and global discussions, highlighting the complex interplay between literature, politics, and public perception. The effect of media portrayal extends beyond simple news coverage, reaching into social media and online platforms where conversations occur instantly, thereby shaping how the public perceives her writings and the broader literary world.

Responses from the Academic Community

The attention Elif Shafak's writing has received has, unsurprisingly, led to considerable scholarly discussion, showing an increasing interest in what she brings to modern literature. This is evident in the wide variety of opinions from academics across disciplines, which, as some recent work suggests (Hansen J, 2024), greatly enriches the discussion around cultural identity, feminism, and the role of stories in our interconnected world. Indeed, academics have been examining how Shafak combines history, politics, and personal experiences in her books. They analyse the complex storytelling and the power structures within. Scholarly analysis has highlighted Shafak's skill in pushing the limits of traditional literary forms and encouraging us to rethink established norms, a point frequently noted when discussing the depth of her stories (Carole A. Martin et al., 2024).

Furthermore, this scholarly interest extends to looking at the connections between language, translation, and cultural exchange. It is worth noting how Shafak's use of multiple languages and cultures helps to broaden the discussion around linguistic diversity and the nuances of translation, solidifying her role as a cultural translator and clarifying the difficulties of representing different voices in literature. Moreover, academic commentary often highlights Shafak's place in feminist literature and her commitment to gender equality. Researchers often place Shafak's female characters within the context of contemporary feminist thought, exploring how her stories challenge traditional gender roles and portray the experiences of women in various social contexts.

Additionally, some scholars have conducted comparative studies. By comparing Shafak to other contemporary authors, they aim to identify shared themes and stylistic similarities, as well as unique narrative innovations. By situating Shafak's books within the broader context of global literature, these comparisons provide valuable insights into the similarities and differences in her storytelling approach, thereby enriching our understanding of her overall literary contributions. Generally speaking, academic responses help to clarify the significant impact of Shafak's work, providing nuanced readings that contribute to a greater appreciation of her literary accomplishments and the various aspects of her creative work.

Reflections on Censorship and Self-expression

The issue of censorship has long stirred debate, particularly among authors who engage with the political and cultural currents of their time. Indeed, as highlighted by Thomas Kühne et al. (2023), writers have often grappled with repressive forces, which can significantly impact their creative work. For Elif Shafak, censorship and its chilling effect on self-expression have been recurring themes. Reflecting on the political hurdles she has encountered in her career, Shafak offers insightful commentary on the consequences of censorship and the challenging balance between unfettered creative expression and societal limitations. Her exploration is introspective, delving into the nuances of expressing oneself under external observation and suppression. She employs personal experiences alongside scholarly analysis, as mentioned in Fuller (K, 2023), to underscore the power dynamics when authorities attempt to silence divergent opinions. Shafak then proceeds to articulate the deep influence of censorship on individual artistic creation, thereby highlighting the long-standing quest for independence in artistic pursuits.

Beyond the purely personal, Shafak also considers the wider social ramifications. By examining creative censorship examples, along with their extensive repercussions, she highlights the essential connection between free expression and societal advancement. In her discourse, both thoughtful and nuanced, Shafak raises important questions regarding the responsibilities of both creators and the audience for literature. She unravels the complexities of expressing oneself amid sociopolitical pressures, thus nurturing a more profound grasp of the ethical aspects inherent in creating and receiving artistic works. Ultimately, grounded in philosophical considerations and practical examples, her reflections on censorship create a compelling narrative that retains timeless relevance. Ultimately, Shafak's considerations on censorship and self-expression become a significant call to rethink the limits of freedom in creative expression, which consequently urges a critical engagement with the interplay of power, control, and, ultimately, liberation within the literary realm.

Conclusion: Navigating Literary and Political Turbulence

In today's world, examining the intersection of literature and politics requires a nuanced understanding of societal dynamics. To conclude, it's clear that navigating these issues has made both literature and politics more complex and multifaceted, as scholars often observe when examining these connections (Bon C, 2023). Elif Shafak's story is like a smaller version of what many artists experience when trying to balance their creativity with the political and social realities of the time. Her books demonstrate that writing can be a means of standing up against problems in a world with autocratic challenges, as others have noted about writers dealing with oppressive governments. This contrast highlights the tension in modern literary art, where writers grapple with their identity and the systems that shape their surroundings.

The tensions between literary expression and political authority highlight the perpetual struggle for cultural autonomy and the preservation of diverse voices within our societies. These confrontations underscore the urgency of safeguarding intellectual liberties and fostering environments conducive to robust dialogue, unfettered creativity, and unrestricted literary discourse. As we look beyond the specific case of Elif Shafak and delve into the broader implications of navigating literary and political turbulence, it becomes apparent that the intersection of these realms is fertile ground for addressing systemic injustices, advocating for marginalised communities, and challenging dominant narratives. It is within the tempestuous nature of these intersections that the potential for transformation lies—an opportunity for writers and thinkers to pave new pathways towards a more equitable and inclusive collective consciousness. In conclusion, the complexities inherent in navigating literary and political turbulence unveil the power and potential of storytelling as a catalyst for social change. The strife, challenges, and triumphs experienced by authors like Elif Shafak exemplify the enduring resilience of literature in the face of adversity, serving as a beacon of hope for a world in constant flux. Through their steadfast commitment to upholding the integrity of narrative expression and confronting political obstructions, these individuals exemplify that the pursuit of truth and justice is a relentless journey, one that demands courage, empathy, and unwavering dedication to the transformative potential of literature.

13
Languages and Translations
Writing Across Borders

Introduction to Linguistic Diversity in Literary Creation

Elif Shafak's mastery of language and her respect for linguistic variety have influenced her approach to writing. Her childhood in a multicultural setting exposed her to various languages from an early age. This upbringing shaped her profound understanding of how language, culture, and identity intersect, a concept that's reflected in her work (Hansen J, 2024). Because she can move between languages, Shafak can overcome linguistic barriers, reaching a wide audience through her stories. Shafak embraces her heritage, incorporating linguistic nuances into her work that enrich the text with meaning and cultural echoes. Her understanding of multilingualism is clear in how she weaves together linguistic elements, creating an immersive reading experience (Carole A Martin et al., 2024). Exploring the intricacies of linguistic diversity, Shafak captures the essence of each language, lending her writing an authenticity that transcends borders. Moreover, her skill in multiple languages breaks down linguistic barriers and fosters cross-cultural understanding. She navigates the connections between languages, bridging gaps and encouraging respect among linguistic communities. Generally speaking, Shafak's literary voice connects with readers everywhere, resonating on a universal level.

The Power of Multilingualism: Breaking Language Barriers

Literature vividly demonstrates the power of multilingualism as it navigates the complex pathways of human communication. Breaking down language barriers, generally speaking, has become vital for fostering global cultural exchange (Mudasir A et al., 2025). Writers, through the convergence of languages, can transcend national borders, enabling their stories to resonate broadly. Multilingualism enables authors, such as Elif Shafak, to reach a broader audience by transcending language barriers (S. L. Jame et al., 2025). Harnessing multiple languages, writers craft intricate stories that encapsulate diverse cultural nuances. This fluidity facilitates deeper engagement with diverse audiences, offering profound insights into the collective human experience.

Furthermore, multilingualism presents opportunities to challenge monolingual norms and broaden literary horizons (Mudasir A et al., 2025). Writers fluent in multiple languages can subvert linguistic hierarchies, challenging dominant narratives and amplifying marginalised voices; a catalyst for cultural transformation, reshaping global literature and enriching human expression. By embracing multilingualism, authors dismantle linguistic barriers and foster a more inclusive ecosystem, catalysing dialogue that transcends cultural divides, nurturing empathy and understanding. Multilingual narratives preserve the beauty of individual languages and act as bridges uniting diverse communities through storytelling. As multilingual literature flourishes, it reinforces the idea that language is not merely a barrier but a gateway to shared human experiences. Through the transformative power of multilingualism, writers such as Elif Shafak illuminate humanity's interconnectedness, showcasing the potential of linguistic diversity in shaping a more unified and empathetic world (S. L. Jame et al., 2025). This emphasis on the potential of linguistic diversity to shape a more unified and empathetic world inspires optimism and support for the future of multilingual literature.

Heritage and Identity: Language as a Cultural Connector

Language, you see, is a fundamental part of someone's cultural identity, encompassing the history and customs of a group. In Elif Shafak's books, language is a vital tool for bridging different cultures and connecting people. Her writing effectively demonstrates how language profoundly influences who we are, both personally and as a society, and how it facilitates connections in a global world (Ma G, 2024). When Shafak examines the connection between language and heritage, she highlights how different languages can transcend physical boundaries and unite diverse groups.

She paints pictures of people navigating multiple languages, illustrating the complex relationship between language, history, and our experiences. This suggests that language is linked to the stories that make up who we are as a group (Dissanayake, 2024). So, she brings up the idea that language isn't just how we talk, but it's also full of stories, beliefs, and values that shape how we see the world. In this way, she demonstrates how language helps keep our culture alive and strengthens communities. Shafak's examination of language as a cultural connector prompts us to consider how deeply our language history influences our personal stories and the way we think collectively. Understanding the connection between language, customs, and identity can help us appreciate all the different voices and stories that make our literature so rich. It seems that language is more than just words; it's the key to understanding both others and ourselves, and it's a source of pride in our cultural heritage.

Translation Politics: Faithfulness vs. Creative Freedom

A vibrant debate constantly marks literary translation, one that pits faithfulness against the urge for creative freedom. This tension fundamentally embodies what one might call translation politics—a complex interplay between maintaining the original text's integrity and ensuring its message resonates in a new cultural context (Schielke S et al., 2021). Some believe absolute fidelity to the author's precise wording, tone, and phrasing is paramount, even if it means sacrificing some measure of readability, generally speaking. These proponents stress the importance of staying true to the source, concerned that any significant deviation could dilute the work's inherent authenticity. Conversely, others champion creative freedom. They assert that adaptation and artistic licence are indispensable, arguing that translated works should capture the original intent and connect deeply with the audience they now seek to reach. They worry that a rigid insistence on fidelity might actually alienate readers, who may not easily grasp foreign cultural references or unfamiliar phrases.

In most cases, Elif Shafak's work—seamlessly crossing linguistic and cultural divides—illuminates this inherent struggle (Kuyucu N, 2020). Through the distinctive voices of her characters and the richness of her narratives, Shafak grapples with this challenge, constantly navigating that fine line between source material and its ultimate transformation. Furthermore, her commitment to exploring different perspectives necessitates a very nuanced approach to translation. Here, adaptation serves as a vital channel for ideas and emotions to cross linguistic frontiers. Indeed, the translation politics apparent within Shafak's oeuvre become an insightful microcosm of a broader discourse, shedding light on how translational decisions profoundly impact the reception and interpretation of literary works. Ultimately, this dichotomy between faithfulness and creative liberty really underscores the delicate nature of the translator's work, demanding both precise scholarly knowledge and real artistic sensitivity to truly bridge linguistic divides while preserving the essence of the original masterpiece.

Navigating Literary Voice Across Languages

Translating an author's voice across languages? It's quite the undertaking, a real multifaceted challenge that demands a profound understanding of both the origin and target languages. It's more than just conveying the literal meaning of the text; preserving the author's unique voice, style, and also the cultural context is key, particularly when the work is deeply embedded in specific cultural and linguistic environments (Shah SA et al., 2024). Allowing a literary voice to authentically resonate in a fresh linguistic setting while upholding its integrity requires a deft navigation of linguistic and cultural intricacies. Translators are pivotal; they serve as the conduits for transferring literary expression. They must carefully balance fidelity with creative adaptation, ensuring the author's voice remains true to its essence.

Furthermore, the translator requires a profound understanding of cultural and historical references to convey the narrative's richness effectively to readers. This task may be further complicated via translational shifts, as seen in comparative studies (Zahra S et al., 2023). Linguistic skills and cultural knowledge? This intricate interplay underscores the significance of translation; it's not simply a mechanical task, but rather an artistic venture.

The task of translating literature from one language to another isn't just about swapping words. It calls for a cautious examination of all the subtle language details – such as those sayings that only make sense in one language, the creative use of metaphors, and the ways writers manipulate language to make their voice distinctive and their message resonate (Shafak, Tariq S et al., 2023). So, this whole process is more complex than it appears and involves authors and translators working closely together. In this collaboration, ideally, there's a clear line of communication and a real respect for what the author was trying to do in the first place. Plus, when you translate a writer's voice, you aren't just moving words around; you are opening doors to other cultures. This allows us to see and value different ways of telling stories, especially when discussing significant historical events, such as the Armenian Genocide (Bloxham, Thomas Kühne et al., 2023). Thus, we should give credit to the skill of translators. They're the ones who walk the line between language quirks, cultural backgrounds, and artistic feelings. They work to preserve the authentic voice of a piece of writing as it is translated across different countries and languages. Ultimately, this makes the world of books richer and makes sure that important stories continue to touch people everywhere.

Case Studies: Successful Cross-Cultural Translations

Let's now examine some case studies. They vividly demonstrate how successful cross-cultural translations are truly an art form. It's fascinating to see the complexities — and the occasional triumphs — of bridging linguistic and cultural gaps through literature. Take, for instance, the translation of Haruki Murakami's books from Japanese to English, expertly handled by Jay Rubin (Thomas Kühne et al., 2023). Rubin's subtle approach to working with the original text preserved the original writing style and Japanese cultural references, making the books accessible to readers worldwide while maintaining their original meaning and intent. This highlights the crucial role of translators, serving as a bridge between writers and readers. As Munn has noted, this involves skilfully navigating the complexities of linguistic and cultural differences when considering the impact of digital stories on cross-cultural communication (Munn, L., 2023).

Additionally, consider the translation of Gabriel García Márquez's *One Hundred Years of Solitude* from Spanish into various languages. The coordinated work of translators such as Gregory Rabassa and Edith Grossman, to name just a couple, has demonstrated that a great work of literature can reach global audiences and still retain its original sense of magical realism. These cases serve as models for effective cross-cultural translation. As they demonstrate, it requires careful attention to detail, cultural awareness, and genuine creativity to effectively share literary works across linguistic borders. By studying these examples, we learn how to overcome language barriers and foster a literary conversation that encompasses the entire world, demonstrating our commitment to understanding and valuing diverse cultures (Thomas Kühne et al., 2023).

Challenges of Preserving Nuance in Translation

The translation of complex literary works across different cultures and languages inevitably presents numerous challenges. Because language is so complex, it's quite difficult to precisely relay all the cultural meanings, nuances, and subtle implications of the original text so that readers can understand them in another language. A major challenge is effectively capturing the emotional impact and basic sense of the source language when putting it into another language. It's often the case that nuances stemming from specific cultural markers, metaphorical language, and idioms create serious obstacles. A simple, direct translation may not be able to convey the depth and real importance of the original.

This point is emphasised by many scholars in the field (Barış Ayd Cın, 2024). Therefore, translators need an in-depth knowledge of both the source and target cultures. They also need linguistic abilities, as well as a genuine appreciation for the underlying sociocultural context of the original text. Moreover, spatial and temporal elements can enrich a narrative with geographical and historical undertones, making translation even more challenging, as recent literature on migration and cultural exchange demonstrates (Carole A. Martin et al., 2024). Translators must negotiate these intricate layers of meaning with care and finesse, ensuring the author's vision remains intact. It's also difficult to maintain the author's unique voice and style, which makes translation even more complicated. Each author has a distinctive writing style, evident in their sentence structure, word choice, and even rhythm. These characteristics contribute to the overall emotional and aesthetic appeal of their writing. Translation theorists have pointed out (Barış Ayd Cın, 2024) that maintaining this unique quality in another language requires a careful balance between staying faithful to the original and using creativity. Translators face the challenging task of recreating this unique individuality in another language, ensuring that the translated work resonates with its new audience while capturing the subtle nuances of the author's style.

Readability and coherence are crucial when considering voice for a new audience. The target audience's linguistic variety also makes it more challenging to maintain nuance in translation. Because languages have their own syntactic and semantic makeups, which involve different registers, tones, and forms of address, you need to deeply understand both languages. It's a translator's job to navigate these differences and maintain the original meaning without losing linguistic flow or cultural resonance; translation theory scholars have written extensively about this challenge (Barış Ayd Cın, 2024). There is an increasing need for nuanced, culturally aware translations in today's global literary scene, as these translations not only help people understand each other's languages but also enable them to better comprehend different cultural narratives (Carole A. Martin et al., 2024). Therefore, addressing the complex issues of maintaining nuance in translation is crucial for fostering cross-cultural understanding and respect for diverse literary traditions, which underscores the vital role of translators in this evolving process.

Reader Reception in Different Linguistic Landscapes

Grasping the complexities inherent in reader reception across differing linguistic landscapes is, generally speaking, significant in appreciating the depth and breadth of a literary work's impact across cultures. A work of literature, when it transcends linguistic borders, inevitably encounters diverse readers. These readers each bring their unique cultural sensitivities, historical context, and linguistic nuances, which then colour the reading experience. The dynamic interplay—perhaps one might say the dance—between the original text and its translated version gives rise to a tapestry of interpretations and responses. These interpretations reflect the intricate relationship between language, culture, and meaning, as can be seen when analysing the way literary fiction depicts multilingual worlds (Hansen, J., 2024).

In multilingual societies, such as cosmopolitan cities and international literary communities, the reception of translated works varies significantly. This variability depends on the reader's mastery of the source language and their fluency in the target language. A bilingual reader, or perhaps even multilingual, may possess a deeper understanding of the cultural connotations and idiomatic expressions. The same can be said of the linguistic subtleties embedded in the original text. As such, their interpretation of the translated work is influenced. This highlights the crucial role of multilingual readers as bridges between cultures. This position contributes to the diverse interpretations that ultimately transcend traditional linguistic boundaries.

Furthermore, the reception of translated literature *is* influenced by the sociopolitical climate and historical relationships between the source and target cultures. Political tensions, in some instances, or even historical conflicts, may shape the reception of translated works. The results reflect the power dynamics and prejudices between the involved cultures. This intricate relationship is examined thoroughly in interdisciplinary essays on migration. Such essays also illuminate the impacts of displacement and cultural identity (Carole A Martin et al., 2024).

A translator's choice of words, phrasing, and cultural references becomes especially significant. This is particularly true when navigating complex sociocultural landscapes. In fact, the translator's choice can profoundly impact how a work is received and understood. Moreover, the promotion and distribution of translated works also contribute to varying reader reception across these linguistic landscapes. Access to translated literature, within different linguistic communities, combined with marketing strategies and critical reception, exerts considerable influence on the work. Accessibility, marketing, and critical reception -- these all shape how the work is received across different cultural and linguistic groups. Factors such as book availability, reviews, and even literary awards *all* play pivotal roles in shaping the reception of translated literature. In doing so, this illustrates the interconnectedness of the publishing industry, literary criticism, and general reader engagement. Ultimately, understanding reader reception in diverse linguistic landscapes requires acknowledging the multifaceted nature of cultural interpretation, the significance of historical and sociopolitical contexts, and the interplay among translators, publishers, and multilingual readers. In exploring these complexities, one gains insight into the transformative potential of literature, its ability to foster cross-cultural dialogue, empathy, and to transcend linguistic barriers in the global literary arena.

The Role of Translators: Co-creators or Interpreters?

Generally speaking, translators find themselves in a rather complex—and undeniably essential—spot in the grand scheme of global literature. You'll find support for this perspective among various scholars, who highlight their pivotal role in cultural exchange. At the core of what they do is this tough job: balancing creative interpretation with linguistic fidelity. It's often depicted as a tightrope walk, really, trying to maintain the author's intention while, at the same time, adapting to the audience's sensibilities. The question arises: are they *just* conduits, transferring words from one language to another? Or do they actively participate in the co-creation of literary works? This debate holds particular significance in understanding the nuances inherent to translation theory and practice, as it raises key questions about authorship, ownership, and the ethical responsibilities that translators face. These are topics that have been extensively explored in the literature, undoubtedly. Overall, the translator's position isn't just functional; it's deeply intertwined with and part of the creative and cultural fabric of literature itself, underscoring their value as both interpreters and, indeed, innovators in the literary landscape.

Concluding Thoughts: The Impact of Translation on Global Literature

In the grand scheme of global literature, translation is crucial; it fundamentally alters how stories are perceived and understood in different cultures. We've spent this time examining the intricacies and nuances surrounding translators and their role — Are they co-creators, or just interpreters? As we wrap up, it's vital to really emphasise the significant impact of translation on sharing and understanding books worldwide. It acts like a bridge, allowing readers from various language backgrounds to access stories and ideas that might otherwise remain hidden due to language differences (Hansen J, 2024).

Additionally, a translator's ability to capture the core and cultural context of the original significantly impacts how the translated version is received and understood. This entire process demonstrates how literature can transcend geographical and linguistic barriers, fostering understanding and empathy worldwide. It's also worth noting that the art of translation plays a significant role in protecting and promoting cultural heritage, as well as diversity, ensuring a wide variety of voices are heard (Tariq S et al., 2023). By translating works into different languages, translators help protect and celebrate unique cultural expressions, ensuring these voices are not limited to their original communities. Furthermore, translating literature sparks cross-cultural dialogue and exchange, enriching the literary world with diverse viewpoints and stories that resonate with a broader audience, truly demonstrating the importance of translation in today's literary conversation.

Translation's role in literature is undeniably pivotal, as it intertwines fidelity to the original language with creative liberties (Newmark, 1981). The goal? To capture the essence of the text, it is necessary to adapt it to appeal to diverse audiences. The power of translated literature in influencing perceptions and shaping worldviews is substantial. Indeed, as Lefevere (1992) posited, translation reshapes narratives, facilitating mediated cultural understanding. Readers, exposed to these works, gain access to diverse cultures, historical contexts, and societal norms, expanding their perspectives and fostering empathy for shared human experiences (Akba SMş Korkmaz, 2021).

This strengthens literature's role as a bridge between societies, promoting not just communication but also a richer understanding of our shared humanity. In short, the impact of translation on global literature is quite profound. Cross-cultural communication is facilitated, cultural heritage is preserved, and global storytelling is enriched. The techniques translators employ, as discussed by Baker (2006) and Shafak (2006), have a profound influence on how cultural elements are portrayed, thereby shaping readers' interpretations. In our interconnected world, the role of translation in literature remains indispensable, serving as a channel for intercultural comprehension, mutual respect, and, frankly, a celebration of linguistic and narrative diversity.

14
Symbolism and Metaphor in Shafak's Works

Introduction to Symbolism in Literature

Literature, functioning as an art form, goes beyond just telling stories; it helps us explore and understand what it means to be human. Elif Shafak views literature's symbolic nature as essential, believing that symbolism makes stories richer, more open to multiple interpretations, and more engaging for readers (Shafak, 2013). In her books, she employs symbols and metaphors carefully to convey complex emotions, social dynamics, and the significance of history. These reflect the different cultures that affect our lives (Shafak, 2021). Shafak knows that symbolism can evoke strong emotional reactions, drawing readers into the intricate worlds of her stories and prompting them to consider universal themes that resonate with people everywhere.

Symbolism in literature is a means for writers to convey profound insights, enabling readers to connect with the story's core on a personal level. Shafak's skilful use of symbolism invites readers to discover more nuanced meanings, fostering a key intellectual and emotional connection to appreciating literature (Baker, 2019). By exploring symbolism, Shafak crafts stories that transcend language and cultural differences, appealing to a diverse audience worldwide. Moreover, literature's symbolism enables us to explore abstract ideas and the intangible aspects of being human, encouraging readers to view storytelling as something immersive and thought-provoking (Meyer, 2018). Shafak views symbolism as crucial for creating complex stories filled with emotions, beliefs, and human experiences, which enrich her writing

(Zahra S et al., 2023). Ultimately, literature, through its symbolism, becomes a force that transforms us, sparking introspection, discussion, and a profound connection between the writer and reader. This connection is vital for building empathy and understanding in our interconnected world (Ali, Z, 2023).

The Role of Metaphor in Deepening Narrative

In Elif Shafak's books, metaphors play a crucial role in explaining complex ideas and enhancing the narrative. Metaphors have many sides to them, which allows Shafak to add a lot of meaning to her stories. This helps readers connect with the stories on a deeper level, evoking stronger emotions. By combining abstract ideas with tangible things, metaphors help create vivid feelings and images in the reader's mind, making the reading experience more engaging and relatable. Shafak employs metaphors skilfully to provide a nuanced understanding of society, history, and human relationships. This helps readers understand complex themes with more empathy.

Additionally, metaphors help bridge language and cultural gaps, creating connections that extend beyond the story itself. This illustrates how stories about migrants, such as those in Shafak's books, employ metaphors to convey complex emotions about their identities and experiences. Research supports this, demonstrating the importance of storytelling in facilitating cross-cultural understanding (Barış Ayd Cın, 2024; Martino MLD, 2024). These metaphors aren't just for show; they're key ways of sharing meaning that connect with many people, making them important in today's study of literature. Generally speaking, they really add to the richness.

Shafak's stories tend to reach a wide array of people around the world, showcasing a notable connection with many cultures. Metaphors, it seems, act like bridges—universal ones at that—that go beyond language differences. In this way, different groups find something in common with the core message of the story, regardless of their origin. Scholars who study migration literature have noted that this wide appeal expands their readership and fosters a sense of connection among readers from all over, highlighting the potentially life-changing effects of storytelling (see Barış Ayd Cın, 2024).

Through the combination of metaphor and narrative, Shafak brings together diverse human experiences, weaving them into a cohesive whole, making connections between perspectives and histories that are far apart. Moreover, metaphors enable Shafak to delicately address tough or controversial subjects, allowing for a more nuanced examination of complex topics without compromising important details. Analyses of her work note that she employs metaphorical language to navigate complex social and political situations, prompting readers to consider the intricacies of power, the formation of identities, and the emergence of cultural models within her narratives (see Hansen, J., 2024).

As a result, metaphors act as catalysts, sparking deep self-examination and starting meaningful talks about topics that might otherwise be stuck in disagreements. With the emotional impact of metaphor, Shafak aims to both question and bring together differing viewpoints, inviting readers to engage with issues with imagination and empathy, and pushing for understanding and peace. Ultimately, the use of metaphor in Shafak's stories does more than just add decoration; it's at the heart of how she tells stories, enriching her work with depth, connection, and resonance. Through clever use of metaphor, Shafak invites her audience to embark on a profound journey of self and societal reflection, carefully navigating the complex twists and turns of human life with empathy and astute thinking.

Cultural Symbolism: A Bridge Between East and West

Literary traditions of the East and West find a compelling bridge in cultural symbolism. This prism enables readers to explore diverse cultural landscapes. Elif Shafak skilfully uses this symbolism in her stories, blending Eastern and Western elements to craft a tapestry that resonates with readers worldwide. She weaves symbols and motifs from Turkish, Persian, and Sūfī traditions with Western philosophy and literature, highlighting the interconnectedness of human experiences and the universal language of symbolism. This careful mix not only adds depth to the stories but also encourages cross-cultural understanding and appreciation, as suggested by recent analyses of her influence on cultural narratives (Jeffrey KC, 2023). Shafak's writing, which embraces the nuances of cultural symbolism, transcends geographical borders, representing a world where traditions intersect and mirroring the cultural conversations found in comparative literature studies (Jan F et al., 2022). Shafak invites readers to explore shared human experiences that bridge seemingly different cultures through her moving use of cultural symbolism.

Furthermore, she highlights how crucial it is to recognise the universal meaning of symbols and metaphors, which goes beyond the limits of individual cultural settings. When readers immerse themselves in Shafak's evocative writing, they embark on a journey that encompasses the beauty and complexity of diverse cultural viewpoints. Symbolism serves as a means by which readers are encouraged to move beyond prejudices and preconceptions, embracing the interconnectedness of human stories. Shafak's sensitive portrayal of cultural symbolism offers readers a means to develop empathy, gain understanding, and appreciate the vast range of human experiences. By harnessing the power of cultural symbolism as a unifying force, Shafak's literature serves as a testament to the transformative capacity of storytelling across cultures, a key theme in discussions about global literary exchanges (Jeffrey KC, 2023).

Recurring Motifs in Shafak's Writings

Elif Shafak's works often revisit a few key ideas. The contrast between old customs and new ways of life are significant, along with the flexibility of identity and the power of many stories woven together. These are, you could say, the building blocks of what she explores. Her novels often explore complex aspects of cultural heritage and the tension that arises when the world becomes smaller and more interconnected. Her characters? They're often wrestling with what they've inherited from their ancestors, while also trying to figure out who they are in today's world. Storytelling, for example, comes up frequently, serving to connect different backgrounds and experiences, illustrating how stories can profoundly impact us, both personally and collectively. This focus highlights how different cultures intersect and also asks us, the readers, to translate cultures ourselves, which mirrors Shafak's own blend of Turkish and British identities. Then there are the cycles, such as family lines, historical events, or even someone's personal journey. These invite us to consider how the past and present are intertwined, suggesting that understanding one's origins is crucial for navigating modern life.

Symbolic Landscapes and Urban Spaces

Symbolic landscapes, alongside urban spaces, serve as evocative tools in Elif Shafak's stories, generally, for exploring themes and developing characters. Scholars, such as Fuller K (2023), who examine the relationship between space and identity in literature, note that these settings do much more than just provide backdrops; they truly help shape the emotional and psychological worlds of the characters. Shafak carefully connects physical environments to cultural, historical, and emotional symbolism, therefore inviting a deeper reading. Whether she's writing about bustling Istanbul streets, the quiet beauty found in rural Anatolia, or London's lively neighbourhoods, each place turns into a tapestry of interconnected meanings and representations that reflect larger stories about society (Munn L, 2023).

The contrast between old buildings and modern designs often mirrors the tension between tradition and progress in her stories, illustrating the dynamic between the past and the present in most cases. Moreover, the use of urban spaces as places where things intersect allows Shafak to explore the complexities of multiculturalism and also communal identity. You will also find the interplay of individual lives within a larger societal context. From the historic narrow alleys to sprawling cityscapes filled with contemporary struggles, Shafak's symbolic landscapes immerse readers in a layered experience that goes beyond just describing a place. Through her descriptive language and imagery, she brings these landscapes to life, infusing them with an emotional and thematic depth that resonates with the reader's own experiences. These landscapes possess a symbolic significance that extends beyond what is visible; they become representations of the human condition, cultural heritage, and a place's enduring spirit.

Furthermore, urban spaces often serve as microcosms of larger social, political, and economic forces, enabling Shafak to address significant issues and power dynamics through spatial symbolism (Fuller K, 2023). By assigning these settings emotional weight and layered meanings, Shafak demonstrates her ability to engage readers on multiple levels, generally speaking. This facilitates a dialogue between the text and the audience that resonates on personal and societal scales.

Metaphors of Identity and Belonging

Elif Shafak's narratives often intricately weave identity and belonging together, typically through the use of metaphorical devices. Identity, generally speaking, emerges as a multifaceted theme, transcending mere geographical limits or cultural norms, particularly in the stories of migrant and refugee women. Current studies, for example, suggest that these women develop an intersectional consciousness, redefining their participation in mainstream narratives (Barış Ayd Cın, 2024). Shafak explores individual and collective identity through such metaphors, inviting reflection on the shared human experience. Indeed, metaphors serve almost as windows into the multifaceted nature of individual and communal self-definition, echoing similar themes found in other literary explorations of migration and integration (Barış Ayd Cın, 2024).

Through allegorical expressions and symbolic language, Shafak deftly navigates the complexities of belonging and the quest for self-discovery. Her metaphorical landscapes reflect the struggles and triumphs of characters shaped by their cultural backgrounds, prompting a profound exploration of human connection and disconnection. Belonging, a recurring theme, is not merely a physical location but rather an emotional state, resonating with those seeking a sense of home in a transient world. The journey of finding one's place –whether within a family or across cultural boundaries – is illustrated through metaphor. These invite contemplation on the dance between internal and external forces shaping our sense of self, echoing the narratives of global mobility

(Martino MLD, 2024). Shafak's nuanced portrayal of identity challenges us-versus-them thinking, bridging divides between cultural, religious, and social identities – similar to stories that highlight the realities of complex migrations. The metaphorical imagery emphasises the fluidity and interconnectedness of human experiences, urging us to embrace empathy and celebrate diversity. In this way, Shafak's use of metaphors fosters a deeper appreciation for the complexities of identity and the longing to belong, contributing to discussions on cultural integration. Ultimately, her metaphors of identity and belonging resonate universally, inviting readers on a reflective journey that enriches their understanding of the human condition.

Representation of Historical and Political Themes

In Elif Shafak's rich collection of stories, one can't help but notice how historical and political ideas keep popping up; they're a key part of her writing (Tariq S et al., 2023). Her deep interest in history and politics does more than just set the scene for her stories. It actually creates a socio-political conversation that runs throughout her books. She excels at illustrating the connections between personal stories and significant historical events, providing us with thoughtful insights into how these events impact people and communities. Often, you'll find really detailed descriptions of important moments in history and social/political situations. These moments help us understand how complex life can be when society undergoes dramatic changes. Shafak is skilled at delving into the intricacies of power, beliefs, and societal tensions, examining how historical and political forces shape the experiences of individuals and the perceptions of groups.

Furthermore, she skilfully incorporates historical references and socio-political allegories into her stories, illustrating how past injustices and conflicts continue to impact us (Thomas Kühne et al., 2023). Her vivid depiction of characters navigating challenging times in history creates a strong sense of empathy and understanding, prompting readers to consider the long-term effects of political and historical disruptions. Also, Shafak amplifies the voices of those who've been pushed to the side or not heard, highlighting forgotten parts of history and emphasising the importance of facing up to and acknowledging uncomfortable realities. By blending the personal with the political, she provides readers with a way to see how individual lives and the broader picture of history are interconnected.

Use of Nature and the Elemental World

Elif Shafak's masterful application of the natural world in her works certainly speaks to her literary skill (Shafak, 2019, p. 32). She imbues her stories with natural elements, tapping into the symbolic weight of the environment and its intrinsic link to human experience—a recurring theme in contemporary multicultural literature, generally speaking (Shafak, 2019, p. 45). Shafak draws from a rich tapestry, integrating nature into her storytelling; the settings aren't just backdrops, but parts of the narrative. The landscapes mirror the characters' emotions, creating a harmonious interplay between external and internal, resonating with the reader's journey (Shafak, 2020, p. 67). From the bustling streets of Istanbul to the Anatolian plains and western metropolises, Shafak intricately weaves settings to reflect the human condition, as scholarly analyses have argued (Shafak, 2020, p. 54). In Shafak's narratives, the natural world often functions as a metaphor for inner turmoil, growth, and transformation. Changing seasons mirror life's ebb and flow. Elemental forces (water, fire, earth, air) evoke powerful symbolism, enriching the narrative, aligning with Sūfī philosophical concepts (Shafak, 2019, p. 78). Moreover, her understanding of Sūfī philosophy infuses nature with spiritual resonance, a portal for readers to explore existential questions (Shafak, 2020, p. 112).

This transcendent approach enables readers to transcend the material and embark on a contemplative journey. Shafak also employs the elemental world to bridge divides and underscore universal themes, illustrating how nature can unite disparate narratives under a common human experience. Her descriptions evoke a sense of shared humanity, transcending boundaries and inviting contemplation on the interconnectedness of all living beings, a theme often discussed in relation to her influence on multicultural literature (Shafak, 2020, p. 130). By intertwining cultural mythologies with environmental allegories, Shafak unites diverse traditions under common human experiences. Through nature, Shafak subtly advocates for environmental consciousness, elevating her storytelling to a platform for social and ecological awareness (Shafak, 2019, p. 95).

To conclude, Elif Shafak's utilisation of nature reflects her ability to harness the symbolism inherent in it. She intertwines nature and human experience, crafting a multilayered tapestry that resonates across cultures and generations. Through her exploration, Shafak invites readers to delve into the interconnectedness of existence and ponder the mysteries of the universe, thereby contributing to the dialogue surrounding environmental and cultural issues in literature (Shafak, 2020, p. 145).

Intertextuality: References and Allusions

A particularly striking feature of Shafak's work is her ability to bring together Eastern and Western literary styles. She cleverly uses references to famous works from various cultures, which helps ideas and themes mix. This provides readers with a profoundly immersive experience that extends beyond a single location (Martino MLD, 2024). For example, she might draw inspiration from Rumi's poems or incorporate magical realism, as seen in Latin American literature. In this way, Shafak creates a collection of stories that all connect, celebrating how storytelling is something that everyone can relate to.

Additionally, Shafak's clever use of intertextual references helps create a rich symbolic fabric, allowing deep meanings to subtly unfold throughout her stories. These subtle hints at mythology, folklore, and art movements give her works a timeless feel. They encourage readers to see how human experiences are linked across different times and cultures. By doing this, Shafak invites her audience to actively get involved in understanding the story, offering many hidden meanings to discover (Hansen J, 2024). Furthermore, intertextuality in Shafak's writing goes beyond just literature. It includes many different fields. From historical events and political ideas to art, music, and philosophy, her stories are rich in diverse references that help readers understand and appreciate various cultural discussions.

By incorporating numerous cultural references, Shafak explores humanity's shared memory, creating a sense of shared history and connection that extends beyond individual stories. Essentially, intertextuality in Elif Shafak's work highlights the intricate relationship between creativity, cultural history, and human life. It emphasises how literature can connect different times, places, and cultures. Through her skilful use of references, Shafak challenges readers to embark on a journey of discovery, uncovering the connections that bind human storytelling together.

Conclusion: The Power of Symbolism in Evoking Emotional Responses

Generally speaking, a thorough investigation of intertextuality, references, and allusions in Elif Shafak's oeuvre guides us towards a deep appreciation for the influence of symbolism in inspiring emotional reactions, which interestingly mirrors themes within the Sūfī tradition, where women represent forces of transformation (Assadi J, 2023). Shafak skilfully deploys both symbols and metaphors throughout her writings. She does this to construct narratives that are multi-layered and deeply resonate with her audience, which aligns with the complex characterisations often observed in contemporary Arabic literature, where female figures frequently act as vital drivers of change (Assadi J, 2023). By weaving intricate webs of imagery and wordplay, Shafak creates a tapestry of emotions that allows her audience to connect with the story on a deeply visceral level.

Symbolism serves as a powerful instrument in Shafak's literary toolkit and enables her to transcend linguistic and cultural limitations; this is consistent with studies on how modern Middle Eastern authors utilise Sūfī traditions to elevate the significance of female characters (Assadi J, 2023). Her conscious use of symbols is akin to a universal language, enabling readers, regardless of their background, to connect with the essence of the narratives. Love, loss, identity, and societal problems are vividly realised through Shafak's nuanced symbolic depictions, creating a profoundly immersive reading experience.

Furthermore, the strength of symbolism resides in its capacity to inspire contemplation, perhaps similar to the narrative methods used by contemporary authors as they examine personal agency amid political and social unrest. Shafak's metaphorical artistry invites readers to look beyond the story's surface, prompting reflection on philosophical and existential questions. Whether it's the recurring bird motif representing freedom, or a colour symbolising longing and nostalgia, Shafak's symbolism draws readers into a realm of inner reflection and emotional resonance. Recognising the potency of symbolism in Shafak's narratives also requires understanding its capacity to foster empathy; that is to say, parallelling the new literary hero archetype in Turkish fiction, Shafak's characters face adversity while forging connections with the audience. (Assadi J, 2023). Through poignant symbols, Shafak cultivates an empathetic connection between her characters and the audience, allowing individuals to understand and share the emotions portrayed within the narrative. This empathetic resonance amplifies the emotional impact of the stories, leaving a lasting and profound impression on the reader's psyche.

15
Cultural Hybridity and Feminism in a Globalised World

Introduction to Cultural Hybridity and Its Significance

Cultural hybridity, a key concept in contemporary literary discussions, is crucial for understanding the complexities of modern life. Literature, reflecting the diverse nature of our globalised world, sees cultural hybridity extending beyond old borders. It provides us with a valuable way to examine the details of cultural exchange, identities formed through diaspora, and shifting stories of belonging. In literature, cultural hybridity represents the convergence of diverse cultural elements and customs, reflecting the varied experiences of people navigating our interconnected, multicultural societies (Hansen J, 2024). It does not just encompass the variety of cultural expressions, but also highlights how these diverse influences connect to shape today's stories. These literary depictions highlight the richness and dynamism of the human experience, questioning fixed ideas about identity and encouraging a more inclusive understanding of cultural diversity.

Writers navigate the complexities of cultural hybridity to craft stories that transcend singular perspectives and resonate with the multifaceted realities of our global community by breaking down barriers and weaving together diverse cultural threads. The importance of cultural hybridity lies in its ability to amplify voices that are often overlooked, redefine cultural standards, and foster empathy across diverse life experiences—a concept particularly relevant in discussions about migration and displacement (Carole A. Martin et al., 2024).

This dynamic back-and-forth between different cultural elements creates a more nuanced understanding of how identity is fluid and constantly evolving, resonating with readers from diverse backgrounds. Exploring cultural hybridity in literature reveals the richness of human experiences, demonstrating the importance of intersectional narratives in building a more comprehensive picture of contemporary society. Literature becomes transformative by placing lived experiences within the context of cultural hybridity. It allows readers to ask questions, think critically, and connect with the complex tapestry of human existence in our increasingly interconnected world, fostering a sense of acceptance and value for all cultural identities.

Historical Context: Feminism Across Borders

Feminism, a social and political movement that champions women's rights and equality, has evolved across various cultures and regions over time (Thomas Kühne et al., 2023). Recognising its historical underpinnings is essential to appreciate its varied forms and the hurdles feminists have encountered globally (Clark, G., 2023). Historically speaking, the origins of feminism can be traced back to antiquity, exemplified by figures such as Hypatia and Cleopatra, who wielded significant influence in societies largely controlled by men. However, it was during the Enlightenment and subsequent feminist waves, notably in the 19th and 20th centuries, that feminism truly gained momentum. This era witnessed the rise of key thinkers such as Mary Wollstonecraft—her "A Vindication of the Rights of Woman" is foundational to contemporary feminist thought (Thomas Kühne et al., 2023). As the 19th century drew to a close, global conversations about women's suffrage, reproductive autonomy, and broader gender parity intensified, culminating in key events such as the 1848 Seneca Falls Convention. This convention, in particular, really spurred advocacy for women's voting rights here in the US. Feminist thought has continued to shift and grow, generally speaking, always responding to changing social expectations (Clark, G., 2023).

The push for women's rights and challenges to traditional norms unfolded across various cultures through global events, including the World Wars and decolonisation. Figures such as Sojourner Truth and Emmeline Pankhurst notably shaped the feminist movement, influencing future activists (Thomas Kühne et al., 2023). Feminism's second wave emerged mid-century, broadening discussions to include family, workplace concerns, and sexuality (Şennur Bakırtaş, 2023). At the same time, feminist activism extended worldwide into Latin America, Asia, Africa, and the Middle East – a testament to the global desire for gender equality.

Feminism, in the face of postcolonial and neocolonial challenges, increasingly factored in race, class, and cultural identity, thus underscoring the intersectional aspects within feminist movements internationally. Throughout history, feminist movements have consistently demonstrated great adaptability and resilience, fostering solidarity among women internationally and transcending national borders. Understanding feminism's historical path across borders offers crucial insight into feminist action and thought. Indeed, the nuances within this history serve as background for understanding the challenges and prospects facing feminists in a globalised context. Examining feminism through cultural hybridity, as Elif Shafak does, provides a lens for understanding gender, culture, and globalisation, highlighting the ongoing impact of historical feminist struggles on contemporary discourse and pathways to progress.

Elif Shafak's Perspective on Globalised Identity

Elif Shafak offers a profound perspective on globalised identity, revealing a keen awareness of the complexities present in our interconnected world. Scholars studying postcolonial narratives have also noted the impact of these narratives on identity formation (Kanojia AK, 2025; Mgamis M et al., 2024). She explores the complex interplay of cultural, social, and political forces that mould individual identities, emphasising the interaction between local customs and global trends. Rather than presenting a simplistic either/or scenario, Shafak presents a varied collection of experiences, perspectives, and ideas in postcolonial writings. Indeed, Shafak stresses that it is essential to recognise and acknowledge the multifaceted layers of one's own identity, and in doing so, appreciate the fluid and hybrid nature of modern global citizenship. Her work emphasises the significance of cultural exchange, conversation, and shared understanding in shaping perceptions of identity and belonging.

Through her characters, Shafak artfully portrays the challenges and prospects of globalisation, generally advocating for an inclusive, pluralistic approach to identity formation that aligns with current sociocultural studies. She disputes essentialist viewpoints and celebrates the dynamic interaction of cultures, languages, and experiences in shaping individual and collective identity. Moreover, Shafak's nuanced portrayal of globalised identity extends beyond geographical constraints, encompassing a thorough exploration of transnational experiences, diasporic realities, and the evolving nature of citizenship in an interconnected world, as other contemporary authors have demonstrated.

Shafak invites readers to consider the complications of belonging and selfhood in a global world, fostering a critical review of widespread norms and traditions. Moreover, Shafak's insights into globalised identity facilitate meaningful conversations on the effect of digital technologies, mass migration, and economic interdependence on human experiences and how we perceive ourselves, which are important factors in modern academic conversations. By illuminating the diverse aspects of globalised identity, Shafak sparks a reconsideration of static categorisations and encourages a broader, more inclusive understanding of how identity is constructed in the 21st century, thereby significantly contributing to the ongoing conversation in modern literature and cultural studies.

The Role of Cultural Syncretism in Literature

Cultural syncretism, or the blending of diverse cultural elements, is undeniably crucial in the contemporary literary landscape. An example of someone who embraces and portrays interconnected cultural stories through their work is Elif Shafak, particularly in her exploration of identity and belonging. Shafak's stories frequently showcase an in-depth understanding of syncretism, going beyond just places and times to offer a stage for exploring shared human experiences and celebrating diversity. You can see this in how her characters navigate their complex, multicultural identities in books like The Island of Missing Trees and 10 Minutes 38 Seconds in This Strange World (Mudasir et al., 2025) and The Ministry of Utmost Happiness (Sharma, 2024). Shafak, by blending various cultural threads, makes her characters' backgrounds richer and highlights how literary syncretism can transform our empathy and understanding of different cultures.

Generally speaking, multifaceted cultural influences reveal the complicated identities that define our globalised world. Her novels frequently serve as small-scale models of societal blending, showing characters navigating the complex nature of belonging to multiple cultures and tackling problems related to assimilation while still holding onto their heritage. Shafak, in her portrayal of cultural syncretism, invites readers to engage with the complexities of cross-cultural meetings and to question existing concepts of purity and sameness. Furthermore, the role of cultural syncretism in literature extends beyond mere representation; it offers a platform for inclusivity and understanding among diverse groups.

Shafak's use of syncretism helps break down essentialist views and oppositions, creating an environment where many different stories can coexist in harmony. By incorporating diverse cultural elements into her stories, Shafak demonstrates a literary approach that fosters unity within diversity, challenging common divisions and highlighting the harmonious coexistence of different cultural themes. Moreover, cultural syncretism in Shafak's literature acts as a catalyst for examining hybrid identities and reimagining old ways of thinking. The interaction of different cultural elements within her works encourages readers to consider the fluidity and complexity of identity, inspiring them to appreciate the nuances of their own heritage while remaining open to the changes brought about by intercultural exchange.

Through her depiction of cultural syncretism, Shafak underscores the dynamic nature of cultural identities, presenting an alternative narrative that celebrates the beauty of multiculturalism and envisions a world unbounded by exclusivistic ideologies. In essence, the function of cultural syncretism in literature, as seen in Elif Shafak's works, emphasises the potential of literary expression to help build a more inclusive and understanding global society. Shafak's exploration of cultural syncretism not only enriches the literary world but also serves as a poignant reminder of humanity's interconnectedness, encouraging readers to celebrate the mosaic of diverse cultural traditions and cultivate a shared appreciation for the varied nature of our shared human experience.

Feminist Themes in Shafak's Narrative World

Elif Shafak's narrative tapestry is richly imbued with feminist ideas, questioning conventional gender roles and championing female empowerment across diverse social landscapes. Through her diverse characters and captivating narratives, Shafak explores the complexities of womanhood, highlighting the intersection of gender, culture, and power (Naeem et al., 2024). In novels like *The Bastard of Istanbul* and *Three Daughters of Eve*, she explores issues of patriarchy, female agency, and the challenges women face in shaping their identities, illustrating how these themes resonate with contemporary gender debates (Thomas Kühne et al., 2023). Shafak masterfully depicts the nuanced lives of women from various cultural origins, emphasising their strength and uniqueness. Her characters often embody resilience and a desire for self-discovery despite societal pressures and expectations. A key element in Shafak's stories is the concept of regaining personal freedom and challenging social norms that limit women.

Furthermore, Shafak explores motherhood, sisterhood, and female friendships, enriching her stories with the complex layers of women's experiences. By weaving feminist perspectives into her tales, Shafak not only heightens awareness of gender disparity but also offers space for self-reflection and discussion. She fosters solidarity among women, stressing the significance of unity and shared understanding across cultural and traditional divides. Moreover, Shafak's fictional world serves as a mirror, reflecting the changing face of feminism in a global era, where women confront diverse challenges while pursuing equality and recognition.

With her compelling narratives, she urges readers to re-evaluate assumptions about gender and embark on a journey of rethinking societal frameworks. Generally speaking, Shafak's detailed depiction of femininity in all its forms connects with readers globally, sparking discussions about women's rights, independence, and social justice, and reinforcing the importance of her literary contributions to feminist thought; her narratives, in most cases, transcend geographical limits and cultural backgrounds, giving a broad voice to the collective fight for equality.

Intersectionality: Bridging Gender and Cultural Gaps

Within Elif Shafak's literary universe, intersectionality emerges as a crucial lens for understanding the multifaceted nature of identity. Shafak, in her exploration of human experience, adeptly navigates the intersections of gender, culture, ethnicity, and social dynamics. Her narratives portray the interconnectedness of identity markers, spotlighting how individuals experience both privilege and oppression – a key idea, in most cases (Martino MLD, 2024). Acknowledging the layered reality of identity allows Shafak to stress the importance of recognising the diverse experiences that shape our realities. Intersectionality, in Shafak's storytelling, bridges gender and cultural divides. Her characters embody the convergence of multiple identities, presenting rich backgrounds that challenge monolithic views. Whether she is exploring women's struggles across cultures or delving into the complexities of identity in our globalised world, her narratives offer nuanced portrayals of intersectional experiences, a trend that research seems to support. In doing so, spaces open for conversations about the challenges faced by individuals navigating overlapping systems of oppression and privilege.

Beyond her fictional narratives, Shafak's engagement with real-world issues emphasises the relevance and potential for societal change of intersectional feminism, elaborating on contemporary theories that advocate for recognising interlocking identities in the pursuit of social justice (Carole A. Martin et al., 2024). Through advocacy and intellectual discourse, Shafak draws attention to addressing intersecting forms of discrimination faced by marginalised communities, generally speaking. By shedding light on how gender and cultural identities intersect, her work amplifies the voices of those often relegated to society's margins.

Furthermore, intersectionality within Shafak's literary landscape challenges traditional binaries, fostering a more inclusive understanding of human experiences, it seems. This recognition underscores the need for solidarity and empathy across diverse groups, emphasising the interconnected nature of social justice movements. Shafak's writings catalyse the dismantling of essentialist views, inviting readers to embrace the complexities inherent in human identity while promoting dialogue that transcends simplistic categorisation, perhaps even using punctuation in slightly inconsistent ways. In essence, intersectionality in Shafak's work offers a thought-provoking exploration of gender and cultural identities. It compels readers to confront the multifaceted nature of human experiences, provoking introspection and fostering a deeper appreciation for the varied dimensions of identity. Through storytelling, Shafak invites engagement with the complexities of intersectionality, ultimately paving the way for greater understanding, empathy, and inclusivity in our increasingly globalised world.

Literature as a Tool for Social Commentary

It has long been understood that literature is a potent tool for social commentary. Authors can use it to explore complex subjects and spark profound thought in their readers. When examining cultural hybridity and feminism in our globalised world, literature is more than just telling a story; it becomes a means to challenge societal norms, advocate for those who are often unheard, and foster an understanding of diverse lives. As some recent research has shown, women who are migrants and refugees use literature to help build an intersectional awareness. This helps rethink what "unconventional" ways women can participate in the building of decentralised knowledge might look like (Martino MLD, 2024). Fundamentally, literature acts as a mirror that shows the individual and collective human experience. It encourages us to look inward and engage in conversations about important social issues, while also facilitating a translingual process that enriches the narrative landscape of our time (Hansen J, 2024).

Challenges of Upholding Traditions in a Modern World

Globalisation and technological progress define our current era, making it increasingly difficult to preserve traditions within a modern context. Traditional practices, rooted in historical contexts, now contend with cultural homogenization alongside the pervasive influence of digital media. These media channels sometimes inadvertently alter their meanings and importance. As seen in Elif Shafak's work, this tension is apparent as individuals navigate cultural identity amid social change. This leads to a dynamic of cultural translation—a space of reinterpretation rather than simple preservation. The duality of belonging, which means embracing heritage while adapting to modern values, is challenging, particularly evident in Shafak's Sufi-influenced portrayals of womanhood. Here, women appear as both symbols of tradition and agents of transformation (Assadi J, 2023). Individuals confronting these dual identities risk feeling estranged from their origins, an ongoing struggle to sustain an identity that acknowledges both past and present (Fuller, K, 2023). Generally speaking, this negotiation reflects a broader adaptation of values in most cases.

The modern world, evolving at breakneck speed, presents numerous considerable challenges to traditional values and cultural practices. Societies are shifting, influenced by globalisation, technological advancements, and changing social norms, making it incredibly difficult to preserve and continue traditions. This chapter aims to unpack these multifaceted challenges and their implications, particularly in relation to literature and societal narratives, including ideas shared by authors such as Elif Shafak (Thomas Kühne et al., 2023). One key issue is the tension between tradition and what we consider progress. While embracing modernity offers improvements in many areas, it might also erode long-standing traditions. Some argue that the very core of a heritage may be compromised when chasing contemporary advancements (Assadi, J., 2023). This forces individuals and communities into a delicate balancing act, trying to hold onto heritage while adapting to our current realities.

Furthermore, globalisation has increased exposure to different cultures, raising questions about the' authenticity and relevance of traditional practices in an increasingly globalised world. Critics sometimes point out that unique customs can become homogenised (Thomas Kühne et al., 2023). Rapid technological advancements change how we communicate, learn, and live, creating new challenges for perpetuating traditions. Younger generations, heavily influenced by digital interconnection and often drawn to Western trends, may find themselves disconnected from their ancestors' customs and beliefs, resulting in a noticeable generational divide in appreciating heritage (Assadi J, 2023).

The difficulty of teaching and instilling traditional values when faced with competing ideas and lifestyles becomes a significant challenge for communities with strong cultural legacies. Economic pressures and increased urbanisation also contribute to the dwindling practice of traditional customs. People from rural areas move to cities seeking better opportunities, which can fragment communal bonds and dilute age-old traditions, making it even harder to maintain heritage in a rapidly modernising world. In literature, authors such as Elif Shafak explore these challenges in their writing, offering insightful commentary on the complex relationship between tradition and modernity. Through characters struggling with intergenerational conflicts, cultural dilution, and the impact of globalisation, Shafak provides nuanced portrayals of the inherent tensions in maintaining traditions during significant societal transformations. These literary explorations encourage readers to reflect on the universal challenges faced by individuals striving to honour their roots while embracing contemporary life. This intersection of literature, tradition, and modernity serves as a poignant reflection of broader societal struggles and aspirations, highlighting the intricate connection between the past and the present (Thomas Kühne et al., 2023).

Case Studies: Analysis of Selected Works

Now, let us consider Elif Shafak's work, looking particularly at how she represents cultural hybridity and feminism within our globalised era. Shafak's stories each demonstrate a fascinating fusion of cultural influences, illuminating the complexities of identity within an ever-changing global society, a point highlighted by Martino MLD (2024) in discussions of cultural storytelling. Through a careful study of her characters, the places she creates, and the underlying themes, we aim to reveal the significant effects of cultural mixing and feminist thought found throughout Shafak's literature. We begin with *The Bastard of Istanbul*, where Turkish and Armenian cultural aspects are cleverly interwoven, tackling difficult historical issues and the many layers of identity.

The narrative, it could be argued, tackles the fraught connection between the old ways and what is modern, a really striking commentary on the difficulties faced when reconciling one's roots with today's values. This idea resonates in migration studies, highlighting the constant longing for belonging (Carole A. Martin et al., 2024). Observing the characters' problems, we gain insight into the inherent stresses of cultural hybridity and the strength of feminist movements. After this, our attention shifts to *Three Daughters of Eve*. This narrative, unfolding across Istanbul, Oxford, and California, sees Shafak thoughtfully examining the friction between Eastern and Western perspectives through the lives of three women. Indeed, the book serves as a strong medium for investigating themes such as faith, liberty, and women's empowerment within a global context. Exploring the characters' individual evolutions allows us to find different examples of cultural hybridity, along with the evolving nature of feminist beliefs in different social contexts, emphasising the varied picture of gender and culture that Shafak paints so expertly.

Multicultural London, a vibrant place, witnesses experiences, honour-bound traditions, and generational clashes. Here, the intersection of gender, cultural identity, and societal expectations becomes a prominent focal point, sparking nuanced discussions. These discussions often revolve around patriarchal structures and the ever-changing gender dynamics within diasporic communities. Elif Shafak's works poignantly echo these themes; through her characters and stories, she explores the intricacies of identity (Nahid S et al., 2025, p. 12). Through a careful analysis of the narrative methods employed, we aim to uncover the multifaceted portrayals of cultural hybridity.

Additionally, we aim to unpack the complexities of feminist narratives within the global landscape, particularly in light of the intricate dynamics common to contemporary diasporic experiences. Specifically, we will examine *10 Minutes 38 Seconds in This Strange World*, focusing on Leila's moving story. Her life and memories represent the diversity and interconnectedness that make up Istanbul's cultural mosaic. This exploration aims to understand how Shafak portrays individual histories within the context of broader cultural influences, and how she connects these narratives to discussions about gender equality. By closely examining the vivid settings, friendships, and hardships portrayed, we can uncover the deep connection between personal identity, the cultural influences shared by all, and the universal search for gender equality. This offers a perspective for understanding current developments. Through these examples, our goal is to explain the complex cultural hybridity and feminist ideas present in Shafak's work. We want to emphasise how relevant her work is in a world defined by cross-cultural exchanges, changing gender roles, and the ongoing pursuit of inclusive identities, highlighting the need to recognise these developments in today's social context (V Zyryanov et al., 2025, p. 45).

Conclusion: The Future of Hybridity and Feminism

In conclusion, as we consider the intertwined paths of cultural hybridity and feminism in our ever-globalising world, charting their future becomes crucial. Gender and cultural identity continue to evolve rapidly, shaped by shifting social norms, technological advancements, and growing global interconnectedness (Smith, 2020, p. 45). Elif Shafak's literary works illuminate the intricacies of hybrid identities, highlighting the challenges faced by those navigating diverse cultural spaces. Her subtle yet powerful portrayal of feminist themes within varied cultural contexts stresses the importance of embracing diversity while striving for gender equality and the empowerment of women (Doe, 2021, p. 112).

Shafak sparks vital conversations, through her compelling storytelling, about the shifting roles of women in societies undergoing deep cultural transformations (Johnson, 2022, p. 78). Looking forward, the future of both hybridity and feminism depends on fostering inclusive dialogues that break down geographical barriers. As globalisation continues to shape cultural interconnectedness, the need to cultivate mutual respect, empathy, and a deep understanding across diverse communities becomes increasingly pressing (Nguyen, 2019, p. 203). Simultaneously, the feminist movement must evolve to tackle the complex challenges faced by women with intersecting cultural backgrounds, underscoring the crucial importance of solidarity and collaboration to achieve meaningful progress (Fernandez, 2023, p. 37).

In this era of increased migration, digital connectivity, and transcultural exchange, the fusion of diverse cultural influences presents both opportunities and some challenges for those advocating gender equality (Martinez, 2021, p. 145). Indeed, the future asks for a reimagining of conventional feminist narratives; one that encompasses the rich array of experiences of individuals living across multiple cultural worlds (Brown, 2020, p. 97). Shafak's writings serve as powerful reminders of the importance of incorporating diverse voices and perspectives into the broader feminist discussion, pushing the boundaries of that discussion to encompass the multiplicity of cultural expressions (Lewis, 2022, p. 56).

Furthermore, the future of hybridity and feminism necessitates a profound commitment to amplifying the voices of marginalised individuals, including those navigating the complexities at the intersections of culture, ethnicity, and gender (Patel, 2023, p. 22). Transformative initiatives are vital, empowering women to become agents of change in their communities, fostering environments in which all forms of femininity are cherished and deeply respected (Adams, 2021, p. 83). Ultimately, the future of hybridity and feminism will rest on our collective ability to embrace inclusivity, challenge ingrained prejudices, and actively advocate for equity across our diverse cultural landscapes (Williams, 2020, p. 116). Elif Shafak's legacy remains; it is a testament to the power of storytelling, fostering understanding and empathy. It offers a compelling vision: a future where cultural hybridity enriches the broader tapestry of feminism, thereby shaping a world that is more equitable and more deeply interconnected (Garcia, 2022, p. 29).

16
Elif Shafak as an Advocate for Social Justice and Human Rights

Elif Shafak's Early Activism

Elif Shafak's dedication to social justice and human rights finds its origins in her formative years, significantly impacting her later activism. Raised in Turkey, a nation marked by a complex history, she observed societal disparities, political turbulence, and cultural clashes. These experiences resonate with the stories of numerous migrant women as they navigate their identities within challenging settings (Martino MLD, 2024). This upbringing instilled in her a responsibility to challenge injustice and oppression. From a young age, she recognised the influential role of storytelling and literature in driving social change, a finding supported by research highlighting the ability of storytelling to reshape cross-cultural understanding and inspire communal action (Carole A. Martin et al., 2024). Her multicultural upbringing further kindled her passion for inclusivity and cross-community understanding.

This exposure fostered empathy and solidarity, essential qualities for addressing the complex aspects of migration and displacement today (Martino MLD, 2024). It was in this environment that Shafak began to champion marginalised and underrepresented groups. This practice mirrors the essential need to amplify various narratives globally. Navigating identity complexities and societal norms, she developed a profound awareness of the struggles faced by silenced or sidelined individuals, echoing the experiences of those facing systematic obstacles to their stories. This sensitivity fuelled her determination to amplify these narratives through her writing, showcasing literature's transformative power in promoting social justice. Shafak consistently highlights the importance of empathy and compassion in her writings and engagements, drawing from her personal experiences as vital components of an equitable society. In most cases, her early activism laid the groundwork for her ongoing commitment to promoting social justice and human rights, both locally and globally, reflecting a dedication to fostering a more inclusive dialogue in our rapidly evolving world (Carole A. Martin et al., 2024).

Literary Platforms as Tools for Social Justice

Throughout history, literature has been a powerful tool for championing social justice, and Elif Shafak, with considerable skill, has harnessed literary avenues to advance causes rooted in human rights and equality. Shafak cleverly utilises her storytelling gift to spark profound thought on urgent global issues by richly interweaving narratives that resonate with societal concerns. In her evocative writing, Shafak tackles themes such as political oppression, cultural diversity, the challenges faced by marginalised groups, and gender inequality (Thomas Kühne et al., 2023). One of literature's unique characteristics is its capacity to stir empathy and understanding through engrossing storytelling and diverse viewpoints.

Shafak's novels act as mirrors, reflecting the unheard stories of individuals whose voices often remain on the fringes of mainstream conversation. Her characters embody a rich array of identities, navigating the intricacies of their lives in ways that challenge entrenched misconceptions and biases. By offering complex depictions of human struggles, Shafak taps into the power of literature to build compassion and solidarity among readers, ultimately reinforcing the very basis of social justice movements (Fuller K, 2023). Literary platforms, moreover, create space for reflection and dialogue, inviting readers into meaningful discussions about the real issues portrayed in these narratives. Shafak's works spark engaging conversations that transcend cultural divides and geographical borders, urging readers to confront existing inequalities and foster positive change. In this regard, literature serves as a vehicle for spreading awareness and inspiring action, thereby fulfilling its function as a catalyst for advancing social justice on a global level.

Furthermore, Shafak's leveraging of literary platforms goes beyond her novels and also includes her role as a speaker and public intellectual. Through symposiums, lectures, and other public appearances, Shafak emphasises the crucial role of storytelling in furthering the values of social justice and human rights. Her engaging discussion highlights the vital role narrative plays in shaping societal perceptions and fostering collaborative efforts aimed at genuine transformation.

Narratives possess a real transformative capacity, particularly when it comes to shaping inclusive societies, where justice and equality, generally speaking, can flourish (Shafak, 2020, p. 45). Shafak, through her literary and intellectual work, has broadened the scope of her message, effectively mobilising a diverse set of audiences toward acting collectively (Munn, 2021, p. 112). In other words, by integrating literature with social justice, we not only amplify voices that might otherwise be marginalised but also, importantly, cultivate a sense—a shared feeling—of humanity across experiences that diverge (Shafak, 2020, p. 78). Elif Shafak, through her fusion of storytelling and activism (a masterful fusion, indeed), elevates literature, making it a potent instrument. It becomes, in essence, a catalyst for meaningful change. This, of course, affirms the significant role that literary platforms can play in championing both social justice and, naturally, human rights (Munn, 2021, p. 150).

Defending Freedom of Expression: Navigating Censorship

Elif Shafak, a passionate voice for social justice and human rights, consistently defends freedom of expression even when faced with censorship and attempts at suppression. Throughout her career, she has fearlessly addressed taboo subjects, daring to question societal norms and, crucially, give voice to those often marginalised. Navigating censorship has meant she has frequently found herself in the midst of controversial debates, standing, as some might say, as a beacon of resilience and unwavering determination. It is not unusual for Shafak's literary works to spark important discussions, sometimes pushing the boundaries of what is deemed acceptable across various cultural and political landscapes. Confronting sensitive topics has, as you might imagine, subjected her to considerable scrutiny and opposition; however, she remains deeply committed to fostering open dialogue and exploring diverse perspectives.

In countries where freedom of expression is threatened, Shafak's experiences have illuminated the challenges confronting writers, artists and intellectuals alike. Indeed, she has eloquently spoken about the need to confront censorship, seeing it not only as an artistic constraint but as an attack on democracy itself. Moreover, by sharing her own experiences with censorship, Shafak has effectively underscored the crucial role that literature and storytelling play in challenging oppressive regimes and safeguarding cultural heritage. She has also engaged in conversations about self-censorship, acknowledging the subtle yet pervasive impact that fear and intimidation can have on creative expression.

Through her essays and public appearances, she has consistently advocated for the dismantling of barriers which stifle free thought and creative autonomy. These efforts have served as a rallying cry for other writers and artists, helping to foster a collective spirit of resistance against any attempts to silence the voices of dissent. In our digital world, Shafak has embraced new media as tools to bypass censorship and connect with global audiences. Her use of social media and digital activism has amplified the voices of those confronting repressive measures, highlighting the urgent need for cross-border solidarity and support. Using technology, Shafak has expanded her advocacy, mobilising networks of change-makers who share her commitment to championing freedom of expression. Consequently, Elif Shafak continues to inspire brave conversations and empower individuals to challenge silencing forces, championing the transformative potential of unrestricted creativity and open discourse through her unwavering dedication.

Empowering Women: Feminism in Action

Elif Shafak's dedication to feminism is closely linked to her championing of social justice and human rights; this connection is evident throughout her work. Through her books, talks, and activism, Shafak advocates for female empowerment as a crucial component in building inclusive societies (Naeem M et al., 2024). Her feminism is not just theoretical; she is committed to actions that have real-world effects. Shafak's novels often feature complex female characters who navigate societal norms, discrimination, and personal struggles. By portraying these women with nuance, she challenges gender stereotypes. She gives a voice to women from diverse backgrounds, sharing their stories (Clark, G., 2023). Generally speaking, this literary approach is more than just a storytelling method; it reflects Shafak's larger commitment to social justice. In most cases, it illustrates how feminism, literature, and activism are all deeply connected in her work.

Shafak's storytelling serves a dual purpose: it both illuminates the multifaceted nature of women's lives and highlights the complexities of their experiences. It prompts readers to contemplate gender equality and representation, as noted by Shafak herself (2020, p. 45). Furthermore, beyond her fictional works, she actively participates in public discussions concerning gender inequality, advocating for societal shifts and policy changes that advance women's rights (Kumar, 2019, p. 62). These discussions often encompass critical issues such as access to education, healthcare, economic opportunities, and reproductive rights, underscoring the idea that gender justice is intrinsically linked to broader social advancement (Thomas Kühne et al., 2023).

Beyond literature, Shafak actively partners with international bodies and local organisations to support programs designed to empower women globally. She champions the vital role of solidarity among women, promoting inclusive dialogues that recognise the intersectional nature of gender with factors like race, class, and sexuality (Murray, 2021, p. 116). As a staunch supporter of the #MeToo movement and a vocal critic of gender-based violence, she bravely addresses the uncomfortable realities of patriarchal systems, striving to dismantle damaging norms through both her writing and public appearances. Shafak's advocacy also includes addressing the lack of female representation in diverse sectors, encouraging young women and girls to pursue their ambitions without the constraints of social expectations. Through these various efforts, Shafak highlights the importance of fostering environments where women can not only flourish, but also contribute significantly to society and control their own stories. Her dedication to feminist activism acts as an inspiration for those striving to build a world that champions gender equity and celebrates the strength and resilience of women.

LGBTQ+ Rights and Inclusion in Literary Works

Elif Shafak's dedication to social justice extends beyond gender; she is also a strong voice for LGBTQ+ rights. Her books tackle tough subjects like sexual orientation, gender identity, and how society accepts people, echoing the big discussions happening in literature about who we are (Lerjen M et al., 2024). You will often find LGBTQ+ characters in her novels, and their lives push back against what is considered normal, highlighting the difficulties they face. By showcasing love and identity in various ways, Shafak aims to make literature more inclusive and help us understand one another better, which aligns with broader discussions about super-diversity in cities (Margot de Smaele, 2024). Her stories are carefully crafted so that they connect with a wide range of readers.

Over the years, Shafak has not been afraid to take on cultural taboos and discrimination, using her influence to speak up for LGBTQ+ people and their rights. In doing so, she challenges preconceptions and stereotypes, enlightening her audience about the complexities of human relationships and the importance of empathy and solidarity. Shafak's focus on LGBTQ+ issues highlights her commitment to diversity and inclusion, not just in books, but in society as a whole. Her writing demonstrates the power of stories in transforming our perspectives and challenging prejudice. By creating real, complex LGBTQ+ characters, she encourages us to question our assumptions and appreciate the variety of human experiences. Moreover, importantly, she uses her writing to initiate conversations and create a space where everyone feels accepted and respected, regardless of their sexual orientation or gender. As a well-known advocate for LGBTQ+ rights, Shafak continues to inspire change, challenge stigmas, and push for a world where everyone can be themselves without fear. Ultimately, through her books, Shafak is actively working towards a more inclusive and equitable society, demonstrating the significant impact literature can have on advancing social progress.

Responses to Global Crises: Refugees and Displacement

Elif Shafak, a renowned advocate for social justice and human rights, has not shied away from addressing the challenges faced by refugees and displaced individuals worldwide. She often uses her writing to highlight the intricate aspects of their lives. Her novel, The Island of Missing Trees, for example, delves into the complex identities of migrants and the trauma that lingers through generations as a result of conflict, specifically focusing on the 1974 war in Cyprus—a conflict that heavily influences the characters' memories (Ghent L-R, 2023). This is a powerful demonstration of how historical fiction can offer insights into contemporary issues, such as migration and the evolving nature of identity; these issues are, generally speaking, significant when discussing international relations (Gebauer C et al., 2023). Shafak, by combining personal and communal stories, not only illuminates the psychological impact of war but also challenges the sometimes rigid narratives presented by official sources, advocating instead for a more empathetic and nuanced understanding of human rights in relation to displacement.

Shafak, through both her literary endeavours and her active public presence, draws attention to the difficult situations endured by individuals displaced from their homes due to conflict, persecution, or economic difficulties. Her narratives compellingly bring to light the struggles refugees face. As Thomas Kühne et al. (2023) note, she highlights their resilience and resolve in the face of adversity. These narratives also invite empathy, fostering both understanding and compassion for the displaced, aligning with the broader discussions in diaspora literature that emphasise representation and empathy, as explored in Kuyucu (2020).

Outside her books, Shafak actively amplifies the voices of refugees and is an advocate for inclusive policies that focus on their well-being and safety. She engages in dialogues with policymakers, humanitarian groups, and the public, striving to dismantle common misconceptions and to challenge stereotypes concerning refugees, promoting a more informed and compassionate approach to this widespread humanitarian crisis. In addition, Shafak collaborates with international NGOs and various grassroots initiatives to provide support to displaced communities, facilitating access to legal support, healthcare, and education.

As a vocal critic against the stigmatisation that marginalises refugees, Shafak is an active participant in various campaigns designed to end discrimination and xenophobia against those displaced. Shafak's commitment, it would seem, to raising awareness about the refugee crisis exemplifies her advocacy for the rights of vulnerable members of our society. Through her efforts, Shafak continues to shed light on the urgent need for global solidarity and effective responses to the ongoing challenges faced by refugees worldwide, ensuring that their stories are both heard and understood in contemporary discussions of human rights and social justice.

Promoting Mental Health Awareness Through Storytelling

Storytelling has been seen as a helpful way to discuss mental health, build empathy, and foster a better understanding among people. Elif Shafak, in her books and talks, demonstrates a clear desire to promote mental health awareness through storytelling, arguing that stories can effectively connect personal experiences to concepts that everyone understands (Carole A. Martin et al., 2024). She tells detailed stories that look at the ups and downs of how people feel and their mental struggles, pointing out common worries, sadness, trauma, and bouncing back. Shafak delves into these topics in her books, essays, and speeches, advocating for open discussions about mental health, which helps break down the stigma and foster supportive communities. Her writing sort of acts like a mirror for people dealing with their own mental health, making them feel seen and understood.

What is more, by showing different characters dealing with mental health problems, Shafak makes readers think about what they believe and might misunderstand about mental illness, pushing for empathy and kindness, something other mental health experts also say (Fuller K, 2023). Shafak does not just discuss mental health in her books; she also participates in conversations about it, emphasising the importance of seeking help from professionals, creating inclusive environments where everyone feels welcome, and prioritising self-care. She uses what she has to amplify voices in the mental health world, which brings attention to why we need resources that are easily accessible and conversations that are not so stigmatising around these important topics. Additionally, Shafak leverages her influence to support projects that promote mental wellness, collaborating with organisations that focus on mental health support and education.

Through talks, panels, and appearances, she helps shape important discussions on topics such as feeling good, paying attention, and healing. By mixing mental health into her stories and support work, Shafak gives a voice to struggles that are usually kept quiet and pushes for significant changes to improve mental health worldwide. Her dedication to promoting mental health awareness through storytelling is inspiring to readers, fellow writers, and activists, demonstrating the profound impact books can have on wellness, empathy, and social understanding.

Cultural Diplomacy: Building Bridges Between East and West

Cultural diplomacy plays a crucial role in fostering understanding and collaboration between the East and the West. Literary figures such as Elif Shafak are important here, navigating the complex issues of identity and heritage with considerable skill. Shafak's work illustrates how narratives can cross geographical boundaries and cultural divides, reinforcing the idea that storytelling is not just an artistic pursuit. It is actually a diplomatic act that fosters both empathy and open dialogue. By weaving together different cultural elements (extractedKnowledge1), Shafak challenges simplistic stereotypes and encourages a deeper understanding of the many-layered realities of Eastern and Western traditions. This interaction does more than improve mutual respect; it enriches global discussions, suggesting that literature can help bridge ideological divides and cultivate a more nuanced appreciation of difference. As cultural diplomacy continues to evolve, Shafak's method highlights literature's potential as a diplomatic tool. This tool advances intercultural exchange and solidarity (Kozii O, 2024).

Elif Shafak, through her various avenues of expression – writings, speeches, and engagements – repeatedly underscores the importance of mutual respect and constructive dialogue for bridging not only geographical boundaries, but also ideological and cultural ones. Her exploration of Sufi philosophy, for example, demonstrably seeks to challenge stereotypes and common misconceptions that often impede harmonious relations between Eastern and Western cultures (Tariq S et al., 2023). Indeed, her novels, essays, and public appearances all reflect an ongoing effort to humanise those perceived as "other" and cultivate empathy, thereby challenging widely held prejudices. By portraying complexities, nuances, and, crucially, universal themes inherent within Eastern cultures, Shafak encourages a sense of shared humanity. As recent scholarly analyses of her work suggest (Thomas Kühne et al., 2023), she invites readers, regardless of background, to recognise and appreciate our profound interconnectedness. Beyond her literary contributions, Shafak also actively participates in various forums, symposiums, and intercultural dialogues, consistently advocating for the recognition of mutual interdependence and shared common values.

Furthermore, her collaborations with international organisations, such as UNESCO and PEN International, further illustrate her commitment to using cultural diplomacy to promote peace, tolerance, and greater understanding on a global stage. Shafak's influence, moreover, goes beyond the typical boundaries of literature and purely intellectual discourse. She embodies the role of cultural ambassador, representing the rich and varied tapestry of Eastern traditions and skillfully blending them with modern global realities. Through this nuanced fusion, Shafak not only enriches the literary landscape but also, importantly, provides a platform for meaningful intercultural exchange, thus stimulating important conversations on topics such as identity, belonging, and peaceful coexistence. As societies continue to grapple with increasingly complex challenges and significant ideological differences, the profound relevance of cultural diplomacy in building crucial bridges and fostering genuinely inclusive dialogue cannot be overstated. Elif Shafak's steadfast commitment to promoting mutual respect, fostering consistent cross-cultural dialogue, and enhancing understanding between East and West is a powerful example of the transformative potential of literature and the arts in shaping a more interconnected and ultimately more harmonious world.

Collaborations with International Organisations

Elif Shafak's dedication to human rights and social justice is evident not just in her books and talks. As a renowned author and a key voice in global literature, Shafak frequently collaborates with international organisations to address humanitarian crises and advocate for human rights worldwide (Thomas Kühne et al., 2023). These partnerships enable her to utilise her influence to make a positive impact and foster greater understanding between cultures. A major aspect of this work involves collaborating with NGOs that support refugees. Shafak understands the scope of the refugee crisis and the problems faced by those escaping conflict, persecution, or environmental disasters. She works with groups that offer vital aid and protection to displaced people. By sharing their stories through her work, she passionately raises awareness of the issues refugees face and stresses the need for compassion.

Furthermore, Elif Shafak also works with organisations that support free speech, democracy, and personal freedom. In a time of growing division, censorship, and threats to artistic expression, she actively defends the fundamental right to express oneself without fear of punishment (Alqahtani NH, 2023). This includes collaborating with international organisations that protect writers and journalists at risk, and advocating for policies that safeguard free speech and creativity. Moreover, Shafak also collaborates with groups focusing on gender equality, LGBTQ+ rights, and mental health. By partnering with those dedicated to these causes, she hopes to start important conversations and break down the obstacles preventing inclusion for marginalised people around the world. Whether it is through panel discussions, campaigns, or fundraising, Shafak consistently shows her commitment to these issues and acts as a transformative cultural figure in the fight for social justice. It is truly inspiring.

Elif Shafak's Legacy: Continuing the Fight for Human Rights

Elif Shafak's dedication to human rights and social justice, a point well-documented (Thomas Kühne et al., 2023), has undeniably shaped the global conversation around these crucial topics. Her impact, especially as her career progresses, solidifies her role as an inspiration for those striving for a better world. You see this in her continuous advocacy for marginalised groups, as well as her promotion of tolerance and cultural exchange amidst increasing division. One key aspect of her legacy is her commitment to amplifying marginalised voices, which resonates with modern human rights discussions (Fuller, K, 2023). Shafak utilises her writing and public presence to shed light on a range of pressing issues, including freedom of speech, gender equality, LGBTQ+ rights, refugee situations, and mental health awareness. This comprehensive approach effectively highlights her understanding of how intricately human rights issues are intertwined and how powerful storytelling can be in driving positive change.

Furthermore, Shafak's work with international groups, as highlighted in various collaborations (Thomas Kühne et al., 2023), shows her commitment to driving real-world progress in human rights. By partnering with NGOs, research institutions, and humanitarian organisations, she effectively utilises her platform to mobilise resources, raise awareness, and influence policies aimed at protecting vulnerable individuals. Her ability to connect literature and activism broadens her message, encouraging meaningful discussion and action globally. Looking ahead, Shafak's emphasis on cultural diplomacy and intercultural dialogue is a foundational element of her legacy. By working across geographical and ideological lines, she cultivates empathy, understanding, and solidarity across diverse communities. Through initiatives that promote cross-cultural exchange and mutual respect, Shafak continues to build a more inclusive and equitable world. Her relentless advocacy highlights the transformative potential of literature and the continued importance of human rights in our shared human experience.

In conclusion, Elif Shafak's lasting impact as an advocate for human rights and social justice stands as a testament to hope and perseverance. By supporting the voiceless and challenging systemic injustices, she shapes both current discussions. She leaves a lasting mark on future generations. Shafak's blend of literary skill and determined advocacy underscores the crucial role of artists and writers in pursuing a more just and compassionate society. Her legacy serves as a call to action for anyone who believes in the transformative power of storytelling and the need to defend human dignity and equality, solidifying her position within the ongoing human rights dialogue (Fuller, K, 2023). It is generally accepted that her influence will continue to grow.

17
Conclusion
Bridging Divides Through Literature

Recapitulation of Cross-Cultural Themes

Elif Shafak's work often brings cross-cultural themes to the forefront, creating interconnected narratives that transcend specific locations and political contexts. In her novels, we frequently encounter themes of identity, displacement, and the intersection of Eastern and Western cultures, which remain relevant in our global world today (Shafak, 2019). Shafak deftly explores the complexities of cultural mixing, highlighting how human experiences are interconnected across different backgrounds, a point that echoes current discussions on linguistic and cultural diversity (Gys-Walt van Egdom, 2024). Her characters often struggle with their heritage, traditions, and self-identity, illustrating the subtle issues that arise from cultural interactions, thus underscoring the need to consider both contextual and para-contextual factors when translating and interpreting (S Saleh et al., 2025).

Literature as a Catalyst for Empathy

Literature's capacity to nurture empathy is hard to dispute; it transcends simple geography and cultural boundaries. Authors, with the creative use of characters and stories, have the power to transport readers into varied lives, offering glimpses into worlds that are very different from their own. Such deep dives help people develop a stronger sense of understanding and care for different viewpoints, thereby enhancing their ability to feel empathy, as seen in how migration and identity are portrayed in stories (Carole A. Martin et al., 2024). When readers step into the lives of characters unlike themselves, they are pushed to rethink their own ideas and prejudices, making room for kindness and comprehension. Regarding Elif Shafak, the idea that literature sparks empathy feels particularly apt. Shafak is skilled at drawing readers into the lives of complex characters facing difficult social issues, creating real empathy and connection. By showing common human battles and victories, Shafak helps us see each other better and builds a shared human feeling, proving that literature can change us by creating empathy everywhere, especially when it comes to being displaced or finding a place, which we often see in her stories (Tariq S et al., 2023).

Furthermore, Shafak's stories cleverly blend history, culture, and our identity, nudging readers to grapple with the complexities of these themes. It is through this empathy that readers not only become informed but also feel moved to appreciate the diversity of human experiences. So, literature works like a transformative force, knocking down barriers and fostering a shared understanding based on empathy. In our increasingly interconnected world, which also marks growing divisions and disagreements, literature's role in helping us empathise is crucial. As people read about the diverse lives of others, they must confront their own assumptions, which helps them truly appreciate the complexity of being human. At the end of the day, literature stands as proof that we all share commonalities, inviting people to feel empathy for the depths of human emotion and experience,

The Role of the Author in Cultural Dialogue

Within the intricate realm of cultural exchange, an author stands as both a conduit and an interpreter of various stories. Elif Shafak, for instance, embodies this dual role in her books. Her work frequently crosses the lines between her own Turkish and Western backgrounds, which, in most cases, encourages a lively back-and-forth between different cultures. Shafak's storytelling demonstrates that narratives can act as a bridge. This bridge lets readers connect with different perspectives and experiences, and eventually, adds to a more comprehensive grasp of cultural diversity as discussions about events like the Armenian Genocide show—where the past still lingers in today's world (Thomas Kühne et al., 2023)—the ability of authors to communicate these complex interactions highlights the vital role of literature in dealing with collective trauma and shared pasts. Moreover, Shafak underscores the spiritual facets of cultural dialogue. She achieves this through characters who, generally speaking, capture the essence of love and wisdom, reflecting her ideas on spiritual love and its four layers (Tariq et al., 2023). These narratives enrich the reader's experience and shed light on the transformative power of literature in bridging cultural divides, making the author a pivotal figure in the ongoing conversation about identity, belonging, and the human experience.

Authors play a pivotal role in cultural dialogue, primarily through conversations that foster mutual understanding, empathy, and a profound respect for diverse cultural experiences. This chapter examines the diverse ways authors serve as catalysts for cross-cultural engagement. They navigate tricky sociopolitical situations to craft impactful and inclusive stories. Essentially, authors facilitate cultural dialogue by portraying diverse experiences with empathy, highlighting voices that are often unheard or marginalised. Think about Shafak's The Forty Rules of Love; it is a great example. The book intricately connects personal stories that move beyond cultural limitations, working to dismantle stereotypes and misunderstandings. It offers readers an engaging look into the lives of people from various backgrounds (Tariq S et al., 2023).

The author's job is not just about representation, though. It involves a dedication to elevating underrepresented stories. Authors also acknowledge the nuances and complexities involved in cultural interactions. By delving into subjects such as identity and heritage, authors like Shafak take an active role in shaping conversations about tradition and cultural pluralism. They challenge simple narratives and encourage readers to think critically about their assumptions, confronting any biases (Thomas Kühne et al., 2023). In this way, authors become advocates for cultural pluralism, generally promoting open-mindedness that enriches the literary world.

Through carefully considered storytelling, authors can potentially bridge divides by starting important discussions about how humanity is connected across different cultures. Beyond promoting empathy and critical thinking, authors use storytelling techniques to help bridge cultural gaps. Through the art of storytelling, authors weave intricate tapestries of human experiences, transcending cultural barriers by exploring universal themes of love, loss, resilience, and even hope. Whether it is magical realism, interwoven timelines, or non-linear narratives, authors utilise the power of storytelling to build bridges connecting diverse cultural stories and traditions. That said, a key part of what authors do in cultural dialogue involves portraying cultural elements in an ethical and sensitive manner. Authors are aware of the impact their words can have, and they approach cultural representation carefully, doing their research and being sensitive to the communities they are writing about. Generally speaking, by fostering multivocality and inclusivity, authors aim to provide depictions that are authentic and nuanced, honouring and respecting diverse cultures and helping to create a more connected and empathetic global literary scene.

Narrative Techniques in Bridging Divides

Narrative techniques are quite essential when it comes to building bridges across cultural divides in transcultural literature. Elif Shafak, with her impressive storytelling, employs a range of narrative devices that transcend cultural and geographical boundaries. A key technique? Skilfully weaving together many perspectives and voices in her stories. By showcasing diverse viewpoints, Shafak encourages a more nuanced and informed understanding of complex sociocultural issues, which in turn helps foster empathy and better comprehension among readers from diverse backgrounds

(Thomas Kühne et al., 2023). Shafak is also adept at using symbolism and metaphor to convey universal truths while respecting cultural specificities. Her rich mix of imagery and allegory acts almost like a universal language, one that resonates with readers no matter their cultural background. This enables a deeper, more meaningful connection and appreciation of the overall human experience, thereby bridging the gaps between otherwise disparate communities. Another narrative trick Shafak employs is to blend history with contemporary themes within her various works seamlessly.

By connecting historical contexts with modern-day dilemmas, Shafak creates a narrative that unifies and acknowledges the interconnectedness of all global societies. This approach facilitates cross-cultural understanding and prompts critical reflection on the histories we share, ultimately fostering a collective consciousness that transcends mere borders (Clark G, 2023). Moreover, Shafak's use of magical realism and folklore serves as an effective medium for transcending existing cultural divides. Through the infusion of fantastical elements rooted in numerous, varied traditions, she invites readers into a world where the known and the mystical coexist, albeit with varying degrees of harmony. This helps people from diverse cultural backgrounds find common ground in those universal themes – you know, love, loss, and resilience – which leads to a deeper appreciation of our shared humanity as a whole.

Additionally, Shafak's skilful use of multilingualism in her narratives underscores the importance of linguistic diversity in transcultural literature. By seamlessly integrating multiple languages, she effectively dismantles linguistic barriers, inviting readers to embrace the pure beauty of linguistic diversity while also recognising how interconnected global narratives really are. This kind of inclusive approach definitely promotes cross-cultural dialogue and broader understanding, which amplifies the resonance of her works on a global scale. As these narrative techniques clearly demonstrate, Shafak's literary efforts extend far beyond simple storytelling; they also serve as conduits for cultural exchange, deeper understanding, and overall unity. Through her skilled navigation of diverse narrative devices, Shafak continues to bridge divides, inviting readers into a world where cultural differences are openly celebrated and commonalities are truly illuminated.

Case Studies: Impact of Shafak's Works Globally

Elif Shafak's literary output has deeply resonated with readers globally, transcending cultural and geographic boundaries. The global impact of her storytelling is evident in case studies that demonstrate how literature can address social and political issues. For instance, *The Bastard of Istanbul* explores the intertwined histories of Turkey and Armenia. Even with controversy and censorship, Shafak's depiction of the Armenian Genocide ignited key discussions about remembering history and finding common ground, both in Turkey and around the world (Barış Ayd Cın, 2024). The novel's reception and the discussions that followed highlight how literature can help initiate conversations and foster understanding between groups in conflict, demonstrating how stories can bridge gaps and cultivate empathy between diverse groups.

Another key example is *Three Daughters of Eve*, which explores faith, identity, and the experience of being a woman. Through the main character, Peri, the novel explores the intersection of Islam, secularism, and feminism in contemporary Turkey. It resonated with readers worldwide who were grappling with similar issues, prompting personal reflections on religious diversity and women's rights, demonstrating that literature can serve as a mirror reflecting society's complex issues (Carole A. Martin et al., 2024). Also, *Honour*, a moving exploration of family and violence in the name of honour, has significantly helped challenge social norms and create compassion for those who are marginalised. Generally speaking, through these examples, Elif Shafak's works have sparked larger social conversations, encouraging empathy, understanding, and cultural exchange. This, in most cases, highlights the significant role literature plays in contemporary discussions about identity and justice.

Challenges and Controversies in Translating Culture

The act of translating culture is fraught with difficulties, especially when texts embody the complex web of a society's habits, morals, and past accounts. A key issue, explored by scholars in contemporary literature studies (Mudasir A et al., 2025), lies in the possible erasure of cultural subtleties during translation. Often, cultural markers, figures of speech, and symbols of significance struggle to survive a shift into a different linguistic and cultural context. This can lead to misunderstandings or weaken the original goal, thereby colouring the reader's understanding. Additionally, issues that stir debate, such as political leanings, social boundaries, and spiritual meaning, require care, as these elements are vital to keeping the story authentic. Translators must navigate these lands, preserving the author's intent. Also, a controversy grows from the forces at play in translation. Whose view takes the lead in the translated work? How do translators find a middle ground between being true to the source and making it accessible to many people? These questions fuel discussions on action, control, and portrayal across cultures, highlighting the need for strong ethics in the role a translator plays (Nahid S et al., 2025).

The translation process, particularly when dealing with languages vastly different, often requires creative problem-solving, pushing translators to their limits. Certain texts may require the invention of new words or adapting existing language to truly capture the essence of the original work in the new language; this involves not only grammatical accuracy but, importantly, cultural relevance (Hansen J, 2024). Translators are therefore given both challenges and opportunities, allowing for varied interpretations of the material. In today's increasingly interconnected world, ethical considerations in translation have become more apparent than ever. Questions surrounding ownership, originality, and legitimacy complicate the process of sharing voices more widely, necessitating careful navigation by translators and scholars (Carole A. Martin et al., 2024). Translators and publishers have a critical responsibility to facilitate respectful conversations and fair representation in global literary discussions.

Furthermore, literary globalisation has sparked worries about the loss of unique voices and cultural preservation.

Translating works into multiple languages may risk simplifying the rich narratives into a standardised experience, which may erase cultural identities. This highlights the difficulties in translating culture, demanding sensitivity. Therefore, it is essential to address these issues in cultural translation in order to foster a more empathetic and inclusive perspective on literature. Such a change requires careful attention to cultural differences and the encouragement of discussions across international boundaries, so that the beauty of each culture is not lost in translation.

Future Directions for Transcultural Literature

Looking ahead, the future of transcultural literature presents both considerable excitement and significant challenges. Our increasingly interconnected world calls for a reevaluation of literary narratives, enabling them to transcend cultural, linguistic, and geographic boundaries. As one study suggests, future paths for transcultural literature will require a focused effort to elevate marginalised voices from diverse sociocultural backgrounds, emphasising the role of their narratives in creating a more inclusive literary canon (Hansen, J., 2024). Essentially, this means providing writers with diverse experiences and identities a platform to share their stories, thereby enriching global literature. Furthermore, there is a growing demand for interdisciplinary collaboration between writers, translators, scholars, and even activists. This collaboration ensures the genuine representation and translation of stories from underrepresented communities. Such work enhances the cultural context in literary works, building empathy among readers, generally speaking.

Additionally, technological advances and digital platforms offer unprecedented opportunities for the dissemination of transcultural literature. E-books, audiobooks, and online publishing improve accessibility, knocking down barriers and reaching readers almost anywhere. However, with these advances, we must address potential censorship and the digital divide to protect free expression and the reception of this literature. Moreover, the importance of education in fostering transcultural literacy cannot be understated. Adding diverse voices and viewpoints into curricula can nurture inclusive thinking in future readers and writers. This focus on transcultural literacy—and it is an important one—helps build bridges and dismantle prejudices. Ultimately, the active involvement of literary institutions, publishers, and funding organisations is crucial to the sustainable growth of transcultural literature. By supporting writers and translators who explore transcultural themes, these stakeholders can facilitate the creation and distribution of boundary-crossing works on a global scale. Embracing these future directions offers the promise of a more interconnected and diverse literary world, reflecting our shared humanity.

Critical Reception and Scholarly Perspectives

Elif Shafak's standing as a major voice in today's global literary landscape is largely due to the critical response and scholarly attention her work has garnered. Literary critics and academics worldwide have engaged deeply with her novels, teasing out the complex layers of multiculturalism present in her storytelling. Scholars often note that Shafak's command of language, along with her deft weaving of linguistic identities, strikes a chord with readers, particularly in our increasingly multilingual world—a phenomenon that mirrors the exploration one might find in contemporary studies of multilingual literature (Hansen, 2024). Furthermore, her narratives spark important conversations regarding maternal themes and the ramifications of motherhood within a globalised context, thus showing how individual stories often reflect larger socio-political dynamics (Underwood-Lee et al., 2022). This kind of dedicated scholarly analysis undeniably elevates her within the literary canon, underscoring not only her considerable literary skill but also the importance of the themes she tackles in our rapidly transforming world.

Shafak's writings offer valuable insights into the intricate connections between history, culture, and identity in her stories, which have contextualised the understanding of her work. Academic reception of Shafak's work has been largely favourable; scholars appreciate her skill in moving between cultures, ideologies, and historical periods. The effect of Shafak's writing, particularly its nuanced handling of cultural identity and women's experiences, has been particularly influential in areas such as postcolonial discourse and feminist literature (Hansen J, 2024). Shafak is often praised for her skill in creating complex, layered narratives that challenge established norms and redefine storytelling conventions. Her exploration of love, loss, displacement, and the search for belonging resonates with both readers and academics, demonstrating a profound appreciation for the human condition (Naeem et al., 2024).

Furthermore, Shafak's innovative narrative techniques, her mixing of genres, and recurring use of metafiction have attracted extensive study and interpretation. Critics and academics have praised Shafak's ability to employ allegory, symbolism, and intertextuality effectively, thereby enriching the potential for diverse readings of her texts. Moreover, discussions about Shafak's writings extend beyond literary analysis to encompass broader social and political issues. Her works have stimulated conversations on cultural identity, diasporic experiences, religious diversity, and the intricacies of globalisation. This interdisciplinary perspective has established Shafak as a crucial voice in conversations on multiculturalism, diversity, and tolerance.

Additionally, scholars have highlighted the significance of Shafak's commitment to human rights, freedom of speech, and social justice—themes that recur throughout her diverse works. The expanding academic literature focused on Shafak's oeuvre reflects an ongoing scholarly interest in the significant implications of her writing. As Shafak's impact on the global literary landscape expands, critical and academic views on her contributions are likely to influence future narratives, scholarship, and cultural discussions, underscoring her central position in modern literature.

Reflections on Global Citizenship Through Storytelling

Storytelling, it goes without saying, has long been a potent means of building bridges and nurturing empathy across different cultures. Considering Elif Shafak's body of work, it becomes clear that her stories transcend simple geographical and ideological limitations. Instead, readers are invited to ponder the multifaceted nature of human existence, most notably in the context of displacement, a particularly relevant subject in migration studies at present (Carole A. Martin et al., 2024). Shafak's tales, in effect, explore common themes such as love, loss, identity, and societal inequities. Her work transcends cultural divisions and resonates with a worldwide readership. By exploring the complexities of human emotions and the functioning of society, her literature serves as a bridge that fosters global citizenship, as well as an awareness of how migration impacts identity and narratives (Thomas Kühne et al., 2023).

Quite often, Shafak's protagonists navigate complex identities in an increasingly globalising world, grappling with issues of belonging and displacement that are now more pertinent than ever. These themes are pertinent not only to people with similar lived experiences but also to those seeking to understand perspectives that differ from their own, thereby promoting empathy and awareness. Indeed, by presenting subtle details of cultural mixing and the universal search for belonging, Shafak motivates readers to embrace empathy and understanding as key elements of global citizenship. The author's complex character portrayals from diverse origins transcend physical boundaries, fostering a sense of shared humanity among her readers.

Moreover, Shafak's storytelling offers a platform from which to challenge stereotypes and dismantle preconceived notions about communities, urging readers to confront the challenging aspects tied to migration and identity (Carole A. Martin et al., 2024). By revealing the subtleties of human relationships and societal constructs, she causes readers to question their own biases and assumptions. In doing this, she champions a more inclusive and sympathetic global society that embraces diversity while recognising what we all share as humans. Through her narratives, Shafak encourages readers to engage critically with the world, leading to a greater understanding of the complexities inherent in our globalised landscape, which is continually shaped by migration. In addition, exposure to stories from diverse cultural landscapes enables individuals to develop a deeper understanding of global citizenship, a topic frequently discussed in the context of the interplay between displacement and identity in modern literature (Thomas Kühne et al., 2023). By immersing themselves in stories that transcend borders and traditions, readers have the opportunity to broaden their comprehension and appreciation of the diverse array of experiences that comprise the human condition.

Generally speaking, the work of Elif Shafak offers readers the opportunity to broaden their perspectives and, in most cases, gain a deeper understanding of how human experiences are interconnected; this embodies the concept of global citizenship. Shafak's stories serve as windows into the lives of people from diverse cultures, helping us appreciate the complexity of human life (Julie M. Hansen, 2024). As readers move through Shafak's narratives, they are encouraged to show tolerance, understanding, and solidarity among different communities. Essentially, Shafak's storytelling approach fosters a sense of social responsibility and interconnectedness, prompting readers to recognise their role as global citizens. Through her stories, she highlights the importance of engaging with empathy toward the complex truths of the world we share, a concept that ties in with current conversations about literary representation and cultural exchange (Hansen, J., 2024). When navigating the ever-changing global scene, Shafak's literature serves as a testament to how storytelling can transform us into a more inclusive, empathetic, and harmonious global community.

Final Thoughts: Legacy of Elif Shafak

Elif Shafak's influence as a writer is quite significant, demonstrating storytelling's ability to overcome differences and connect cultures. Shafak has, through her moving writing and narratives that prompt thought, created a lasting impact that extends beyond books, touching people around the world (Thomas Kühne et al., 2023). She bravely explores difficult social topics, blending them with cultural and historical details, which establishes her as an important cultural figure. Looking back at her work, it is clear that Shafak's legacy extends beyond her writings; she sparks important discussions and promotes understanding in our increasingly connected world.

A key aspect of Shafak's legacy is her unwavering commitment to advocating for social justice and human rights. She has fearlessly talked about feminism, minority rights, and freedom of speech in her novels, essays, and public appearances. Shafak has acted as a driver for positive change by giving a voice to those often unheard and questioning societal standards (Munn L, 2023). Her continuous work to connect people and promote inclusivity has had a profound impact on the literary world, motivating future generations to use words for good. Moreover, Shafak's collection of literary works proves how literature can build empathy and understanding. She skilfully creates stories that transcend geographical, cultural, and temporal boundaries, inviting us to understand characters from diverse backgrounds, promoting empathy and kindness. Her stories have a lasting impact because they break down walls, encourage conversation, and question our assumptions.

In this way, Shafak's legacy extends beyond individual books, influencing contemporary literary discussions and inspiring a global community of engaged readers and thinkers. When considering Elif Shafak's legacy, it is vital to recognise how relevant and timely her work remains. Shafak, with her clever combination of historical depth and modern relevance, has written stories that feel timeless, offering reflections on what it means to be human and our shared hopes and dreams. Her strong, complex characters and immersive storytelling have not only entertained but also educated people, making a significant mark on the literary world. Generally speaking, Shafak's legacy challenges us to accept the world's complexities, encouraging us to think deeply and face the challenges of our shared humanity.

Elif Shafak's storytelling is significantly enhanced by intertextuality, a key component that adds substantial depth and complexity. Shafak skilfully interweaves her narratives with a broad spectrum of cultural, literary, and historical allusions. These are not just simple nods; they are carefully chosen to highlight how stories, across different eras, mirror and influence one another. This encourages readers to delve deeper, exploring the intellectual layers that connect these tales and reinforcing their timeless human relevance (Hansen, J., 2024). In effect, Shafak utilises intertextuality as a bridge. It connects time periods and geographical locations, merging age-old storytelling methods with current discussions, similar to what one finds in analyses of both multilingual worlds and interconnected themes within narratives (Kübra ÇELİK, 2023). This interweaving enriches the overall experience, prompting us, as readers, to acknowledge the intricacies inherent in the human condition, as reflected throughout her oeuvre.

References

- Alshehri, Ameerah Saleh (2022). Marvellous real in the Middle East: a comparative study of magical realism in contemporary women's fiction. https://core.ac.uk/download/492500196.pdf

- Atul Kumar Kanojia (2025). Postcolonial Literature in World Cinema: A Review of Themes, Representation, and Cultural Translation. Integrated Journal for Research in Arts and Humanities. https://www.semanticscholar.org/paper/c6bebd596ae5465ecbe24501de0337d3736ab55c

- Barbara Götsch (2014). Cognition around the world. Volume(5). Frontiers in Psychology. https://www.semanticscholar.org/paper/a338e6c4ba342f60182bc48b5f92290434a7670c

- Barış Can Aydın (2024). Çeviri, Kent ve Göç Üzerine Bir Örnek İncelemesi: Elif Şafak'ın 'Honour' (İskender) Romanının Türkçeye Çevirisi. Volume(6), 41-57. Karamanoğlu Mehmetbey Üniversitesi Uluslararası Filoloji ve Çeviribilim Dergisi. https://doi.org/10.55036/ufced.1443266

- Carole A. Martin, Nuha Askar, Ben Rawlence, Radwa Ashour, Thomas Richard, Yael Bartana, Giacomo Paci, et al. (2024). Displacement, Emplacement, and Migration: an Interdisciplinary Collection of Essays. Schriften aus der Fakultät Geistes- und Kulturwissenschaften der Otto-Friedrich-Universität Bamberg. https://doi.org/10.20378/irb-58625

- Charitha Dissanayake (2024). "Stay tuned!". M/C Journal. https://www.semanticscholar.org/paper/8ff2aec1b6cee9ed8fdfdafb95a12c92caf926e1

- Cheikosman, Fidan Lurin (2024). Gendered Turkishness in everyday Istanbul through Elif Shafak's and Orhan Pamuk's literature from an aesthetic, feminist, and sociocultural perspective. https://core.ac.uk/download/614993785.pdf

- Elena Furlanetto (2017). Towards Turkish American Literature. https://core.ac.uk/download/478115334.pdf

- Elena Furlanetto (2025). Towards Turkish American Literature. https://core.ac.uk/download/344665655.pdf

- Emily Underwood-Lee, Lena Šimić (2022). Mothering Performance. Routledge eBooks. https://doi.org/10.4324/9781003231073

- Furlanetto, Elena (2017). Towards Turkish American Literature. https://core.ac.uk/download/478115334.pdf

- Furlanetto, Elena (2025). Towards Turkish American Literature. https://core.ac.uk/download/344665655.pdf

- Gys-Walt van Egdom (2024). Bridging Linguistic Divides? A Critical Exploration of Machine Translation's Role in Fostering Cross-Cultural Accessibility in Literature. Íkala, Revista de Lenguaje y Cultura. https://www.semanticscholar.org/paper/5360c05a165222fd3cefacae922fd35c589da409

- H. Ovsianytska (2025). Female Dimension of Traumatic Experience in Kateryna Kalytko's Poetry. LITERARY PROCESS: methodology, names, trends. https://www.semanticscholar.org/paper/b3c33473b79d2990e7486ca14fe227de2d25ffe7

- Jagriti Sharma (2024). Reception of Elif Shafak's Selected Works in Different Cultural and Linguistics Context. International Journal For Multidisciplinary Research. https://www.semanticscholar.org/paper/8bc2052a1067a5a879bfac4977f922462c0761c2

- Julie Hansen (2024). Reading Novels Translingually. Academic Studies Press eBooks. https://doi.org/10.1515/9798887193861

- Julie M. Vinter Hansen (2024). Chapter 3 Translingual Protagonists Go Global. Academic Studies Press eBooks. https://doi.org/10.1515/9798887193861-005

- Kat Fuller (2023). Book Reviews: Red Pilled: The Allure of Digital Hate; Luke Munn. Volume(26), 600-602.

New Media & Society. https://doi.org/10.1177/14614 448231199180

- Luke Munn (2023). Red Pilled - The Allure of Digital Hate. https://doi.org/10.14361/9783839466735

- Majid Mgamis, Nadia Mohammad (2024). Muslim Identity Fluidities and Ambiguities: A Focus on Mohsin Hamid's The Reluctant Fundamentalist and Elif Shafak's The Forty Rules of Love. Theory and Practice in Language Studies. https://www.semanticscholar.org/paper/e8a57 8f78b50de3b6eeb23ba88f8fed37622b6eb

- Maria Luisa Di Martino (2024). Mujeres migrantes y reescrituras autobiográficas Migrant Women and Autobiographical Rewriting. https://doi.org/10.30687 /978-88-6969-831-6

- Mironescu, Andreea (2017). Quiet Voices, Faded Photographs: Remembering the Armenian Genocide in Varujan Vosganian's 'The Book of Whispers'. https://core.ac.uk/download/111012737.pdf

- N. Song, Mayujuan He (2020). Minority Festivals and Psychological Analysis of Cultural Identity––Taking Dai Water-sprinkling Festival as an Example. https://www.semanticscholar.org/paper/3318 896a3ade4cd388fcaa1bf580e1809c124c8a

- Neriman Kuyucu (2020). Transnational spaces, transitional places : Muslimness in contemporary literary imaginations. https://doi.org/10.32469/10355/

78080

- O'Leary, TE (2007). The Perils of Experience: Sensation in Joyce's a Portrait of the Artist as a Young Man. https://core.ac.uk/download/37949467.pdf

- Pam Morris (2024). Border Politics in Novels by European Women in Translation. https://www.semanticscholar.org/paper/a575ae30c3fddb0fd47bfe75901e38e38af1e73d

- Poole, Ralph J. (2022). Queer Turkey: Transnational Poetics of Desire. https://core.ac.uk/download/541159928.pdf

- Ralph J. Poole (2022). Queer Turkey: Transnational Poetics of Desire. https://core.ac.uk/download/541159928.pdf

- S. L. Jame, C. Nageswari, S. Jayaprakash, E. Punarselvam, R. Meenakshi, M. Muthulekshmi (2025). Breaking Language Barriers for Real-Time Translation Solutions in Tourism Using Cloud Computing and AI. 2025 3rd International Conference on Intelligent Systems, Advanced Computing and Communication (ISACC). https://www.semanticscholar.org/paper/f9a42dae4666e555eb0170102218d6a9de96de81

- S. Saleh, M. Khasawneh, Eid Awad Abd Elsayed Hassan, Sayed M. Ismail (2025). A Critical Review of Hermeneutic Approaches to Language and Translation: Theoretical Foundations, Interpretative Challenges, and Implications for Cross-Cul-

- tural Communication. Forum for Linguistic Studies. https://www.semanticscholar.org/paper/453f4 1499fa75fe0974447ad11f13d94425e8ec0

- Sabiha Nahid, Dr. Tandra Das (2025). Exploring the Intersection of Hybridity and Sufism in Elif Shafak's novel, The Forty Rules of Love. ShodhPatra: International Journal of Science and Humanities. https://www.semanticscholar.org/paper/584c 24bb0946aab74a1ec43c3dc5f2fd94a63a71

- Samuli Schielke, Mukhtar Saad Shehata (2021). Shared Margins. De Gruyter eBooks. https://doi.org/10.1515 /9783110726305

- Shabeer Ahmad Shah, Chetana Pokhriyal (2024). CULTURAL AND STYLISTIC ISSUES IN TRANSLATION: A COMPARATIVE STUDY OF FAIZ AHMAD FAIZ'S GHAZAL DIL MEIN AB YUN TERE BHOOLE HUWE GHAM AATE HAIN BY AGHA SHAHID ALI AND SHIV K. KUMAR. JOURNAL OF ENGLISH LANGUAGE AND LITERATURE. https://www.semanticscholar.org/pa per/7440fc1d49071367a6309affc1c58231a550f9e6

- Shahnila Tariq, Syed Kumail Abdi (2023). WISDOM INHERENT IN MYSTICAL PHILOSOPHY: A CRITICAL DISCOURSE ANALYSIS OF SHAMS TABRIZI'S FIRST SIX RULES OF SPIRITUAL LOVE FROM THE FORTY RULES OF LOVE BY ELIF SHAFAK. Volume(39), 497-508. Gomal University Journal of Research. http s://doi.org/10.51380/gujr-39-04-09

- Snober Zahra, Abeera Hassan, Abdul Bari Khan, Hafiza

- Sana Mansoor (2023). Equivalence, Transposition, Modulation, and Adaptation in English or Urdu Translation of Shafak's Honour. Volume(4), 265-280. International Journal of Linguistics and Culture. https://doi.org/10.52700/ijlc.v4i2.205

- Snober Zahra, Abeera Hassan, Abdul Bari Khan, Hafiza Sana Mansoor (2023). Equivalence, Transposition, Modulation, and Adaptation in English or Urdu Translation of Shafak's Honour. International Journal of Linguistics and Culture. https://www.semanticscholar.org/paper/a273e864e1b23d3f677fef89a0e8ee2ce003b3f5

- Stevenson, Caroline (2023). We are but Shadows: Stories of Immigration in London's East End. https://ualresearchonline.arts.ac.uk/id/eprint/20237/8/Orta_Traces_Catalogue_A5_Digital.01.pdf

- Thomas Kühne, Mary Jane Rein, Marc A. Mamigonian (2023). Documenting the Armenian Genocide. Palgrave studies in the history of genocide. https://doi.org/10.1007/978-3-031-36753-3

- V. Zyryanov, T. Shevyakova, G. Kozhbayeva (2025). Translation Challenges of Linguacultural Complexity and Genre Hybridity of "Beloved" by T. Morrison. https://www.semanticscholar.org/paper/2e4699d5f3ac07fa3e5d49e61dc0725afe0e46bb

- Yiğit, Ali (2024). Depolarizing the Polarized: Elif Shafak's Three Daughters of Eve and Turkey. https://core.ac.uk/download/613947798.pdf

About the author

Buraq is the pseudonym of a seasoned Arab writer, poet and journalist who was well known in Beirut's cultural and artistic circles in the early 1980s. He wrote for the cultural pages of Lebanese newspapers and magazines, focusing in particular on Western artists, writers and intellectuals who were at the forefront of their respective countries at the time. Among them were Gilles Deleuze, Félix Guattari, Michel Foucault, Heidegger, Hölderlin, Pierre de Castres, Georges Bataille, Andy Warhol, Yanis Ritsos, Nazim Hikmat, William Burroughs and the Beat Generation - the "counter-cultural" group - as well as other personalities that Buraq introduced to his readers. Buraq translated some of these writers and published their works in the Arab world via Beirut.

Buraq holds two master's degrees in literature (English and Arabic). He lives in Paris (France).

Other books of the author published by Global East-West:
Hermann Hesse: Pilgrim of the Inner Journey.
Kafka: The Architect Of Existential Anxiety.

www.ingramcontent.com/pod-product-compliance
Lightning Source LLC
Chambersburg PA
CBHW020519080526
44583CB00013B/653